A NATURALIST'S GUIDE TO THE

BIR~

FRAS~ ~ILL

AND THE HIGHLAND ~ PENINSULAR MALAYSIA

Geoffrey Davison, Con Foley & Adam Hogg

With assistance from Allen Jeyarajasingam

JOHN BEAUFOY PUBLISHING

First published in the United Kingdom in 2019 by John Beaufoy Publishing Ltd
11 Blenheim Court, 316 Woodstock Road, Oxford OX2 7NS, England
www.johnbeaufoy.com

Photo Credits
Front cover: *main image*: Malaysian Hill Partridge; *bottom left*: Streaked Spiderhunter; *bottom centre*: Common Green Magpie; *bottom right*: Sultan Tit, all © Adam Hogg.
Back cover Red-headed Trogon © Adam Hogg.
Title page Blue-winged Pitta © Con Foley.
Contents page Banded Kingfisher © Con Foley.
Main descriptions: Photographs are denoted by a page number followed by t (top), b (bottom), l (left), c (centre) or r (right).
Amar-Singh HSS 19, 32t, 124; **David Bakewell** 60t, 137t; **Cheong Weng Chun** 49t; **Choy Wai Mun** 41b, 56, 97b; **Muhammad Alzahri Bin Darus** 51, 82, 115b, 153t; **James Eaton** 16b, 28t, 29t, 29c, 30b, 31t, 31b, 33t, 36b, 37b, 38b, 39t, 43, 92b, 94b, 95t, 97t, 104b, 110b, 129, 131, 133t, 134t, 135t, 138, 141t, 156t, 157t; **Con Foley** 17t, 18, 22t, 22b, 23t, 23b, 24t, 24b, 25t, 25b, 26t, 26b, 27t, 28t, 29t, 29b, 30t, 33b, 34t, 34b, 35t, 35b, 36t, 37t, 40b, 41b, 42b, 44t, 44b, 45t, 45b, 46t, 46b, 47b, 49b, 57t, 58t, 58b, 59t, 59b, 60b, 61t, 61b, 62t, 62b, 63t, 63b, 64t, 65b, 66t, 66b, 67t, 67b, 68t, 69t, 70b, 71t, 72t, 72b, 73t, 74, 76t, 77b, 78b, 79t, 79b, 80b, 81t, 81b, 82b, 83t, 84b, 85t, 86b, 87b, 88t, 89b, 91t, 91b, 93t, 94t, 95b, 96t, 98t, 98b, 99t, 100t, 100b, 101b, 102b, 103t, 104t, 105t, 106b, 107t, 107b, 108t, 108b, 109t, 109b, 110t, 111t, 111b, 112b, 113b, 116b, 117t, 117b, 118t, 118b, 119t, 119b, 120t, 120b, 121t, 121b, 123t, 123b, 126b, 127t, 128t, 128b, 130t, 130b, 132b, 133b, 134b, 135b, 136t, 137b, 139b, 140b, 141b, 142t, 142b, 143, 145t, 145b, 146t, 146b, 147t, 147b, 148t, 148b, 149t, 149b, 150t, 151t, 152t, 152b, 153b, 154t, 155t, 155b, 156t, 157t, 158t, 158b, 159t, 159b, 160t, 160b, 161t; **Adam Hogg** 15t, 15b, 16t, 17b, 21t, 21b, 27b, 28b, 32b, 38t, 39b, 41t, 42t, 47t, 48t, 48b, 50, 52b, 53b, 54t, 54b, 55, 57b, 64t, 65t, 68b, 69b, 70t, 71b, 73b, 75l, 75r, 76b, 78t, 83b, 84t, 85b, 86t, 87t, 88b, 89t, 92t, 93b, 96b, 101t, 102t, 103b, 106t, 112t, 113t, 114t, 114b, 115t, 116t, 122, 127b, 132t, 136b, 139t, 140t, 144l, 144r, 151b, 154b; **Allen Jeyarajasingam** 99b; **Andy Paul** 77t; **John Steed** 105b, **Francis Yap** 90.

Great care has been taken to maintain the accuracy of the information contained in this work. However, neither the publishers nor the authors can be held responsible for any consequences arising from the use of the information contained therein.

ISBN 978-1-912081-54-7

Edited by Krystyna Mayer
Designed by Gulmohur Press, New Delhi

Printed and bound in Malaysia by Times Offset (M) Sdn. Bhd.

·Contents·

INTRODUCTION

Introducing the birds of Fraser's Hill, as well as the Cameron and Genting Highlands, in Peninsular Malaysia, this book focuses on field use for beginner and expert birdwatchers alike, with data on identifying each species, and on its distribution, habitats and habits. Photographs accompany the descriptions. There is information on key trails to visit and the bird species that can be found on them, as well as on climate, geography and habitats. An up-to-date checklist lists all the species recorded for the area and their status within the three hill stations (see below). Under distribution in the species accounts, directions accompanying regional and country names are abbreviated as follows: N (north, northern), S (south, southern), E (east, eastern), W (west, western), NE (north-east), SE (south-east) and C (central).

SCOPE OF THE BOOK

Near the end of this book is the checklist of the birds recorded at Fraser's Hill – the book's main focus – Cameron Highlands and Genting Highlands. These are the three important hill stations along the Main Range of mountains (Banjaran Besar, Banjaran Titiwangsa), running approximately north–south through Peninsular Malaysia. Bransbury's (1992) book is still a useful starting point for bird lists and descriptions of all three hill stations. The three lists are of highly unequal status and should not be taken at face value. They have been powerfully affected by the geography, history of land use, ease of transport and differing levels of interest evinced by birdwatchers in past decades. The list of birds recorded at Fraser's Hill is complete. Fraser's Hill is extremely compact, with a good network of quiet roads, intact forests and a long history of legal protection. When you stay at Fraser's Hill, the forest is right outside the door. Until 1996 there was only one access road, and The Gap (Semangkoh Pass, Ginting Semangkok) at the lower end of this road was a natural stopping point for all traffic. There was a rest house there since before 1910, along with enforced parking because of the 'one hour up, one hour down' traffic system. The Gap formed a natural point for the lower elevation limits of birdwatching, and records from below that elevation are excluded from the list.

No such clarity applies to Cameron Highlands. Although exploration here began at about the same time as at Fraser's Hill, it is a much vaster area, with more limited tarred roads but a huge agricultural hinterland where the forest has been greatly reduced, and it is now serviced by an expanding network of vehicle tracks. Agriculture has included famous tea estates (such as Boh, Blue Valley and Sungai Palas), and vast areas devoted to intensive flower and vegetable production. Some of this is now conducted under huge plastic shelters. Agricultural expansion has been challenging to balance against forest management and legal protection of the surrounding wildlife sanctuary. The control of soil erosion related to farming and infrastructure in such steep, high rainfall conditions, as well as the use of pesticides and fertilizers and the administrative framework, have all played their part. As well as agriculture, the development of water supply and hydro power has added significant new habitats with a different range of wildlife. Lower down the slopes and foothills, a long history of settlement by indigenous people and more recent forestry have resulted in many areas of bamboo and secondary vegetation. There is no obvious cut-off point for birdwatchers to begin and end their observations between the mountains and the lowlands. Getting around is challenging for the independent birdwatcher without a car. Therefore the bird list for this area is less well defined, less thorough, but more extensive and far from complete.

At Genting Highlands (centred on the peak of Gunung Ulu Kali) there is an obvious cut-off point, the tunnel and pass at Ginting Simpah, but this is a little lower than The Gap at Fraser's Hill. The Field Studies Centre of the University of Malaya, at Ulu Gombak, is well below Ginting Simpah, and has a long list of lowland forest birds not included here. From the 1960s onwards there was a single long access road up to the peak of Gunung Ulu Kali. It was easy enough to stop anywhere along the side of the road, and there was a closed older section (the 'old pump road') and a forest trail to the nearby spur, Gunung Bunga Buah. These older sections gave access to plenty of birdwatching at lower altitudes, but the small area of stunted elfin forest near the summit has long gone to building works (Chua & Saw, 2001), and much of the hotel and casino entertainment is now conducted indoors with little exposure to the outdoor environment. Stopping at the side of the road can be dangerous, though there are intermediate places to stay at Gohtong Jaya apartments and Awana Highlands Resort.

Furthermore, an intensive mist-netting programme to study nocturnal migrant birds was conducted at Fraser's Hill during the 1960s and '70s. This provided many data for Medway & Wells (1976) and Wells (1999, 2007). There has been only a little netting of a similar nature at Cameron Highlands (McClure, 1964). This has revealed records of scarce migrants and passage movements of species such as the Tufted Duck (at Fraser's Hill) and Rufous-headed Robin (at Cameron Highlands), never otherwise detected.

The great bulk of information in this book is therefore for Fraser's Hill, with relatively little for Cameron Highlands and Genting Highlands. Differences in bird lists for the three hill stations are only partly due to natural factors such as differences in maximum elevation and forest characteristics, and are strongly influenced by the human factors outlined above.

Geography and Climate

Peninsular Malaysia is a political term denoting all but two of Malaysia's 13 States (the others, Sabah and Sarawak, are in Borneo) whereas the Malay Peninsula is a geographical term including the southern, peninsular part of Thailand as well. Peninsular Malaysia spans approximately 600km from the border with Thailand in the north to Singapore in the south. The Main Range (Banjaran Titiwangsa) begins 50km north of the Thai border, and extends for another 350km south of the border to peter out in lower hills southwards to the state of Negeri Sembilan. The southernmost significant peak is Gunung Telapa Burok (1,176m) at 2° 50' N. The Main Range is not quite straight but forms an arc that, within Peninsular Malaysia, predominantly trends from north to south-south-east.

To the north, Cameron Highlands district, covering 712km², is at roughly the widest point along the Main Range. The highest peak within Cameron Highlands is Gunung Brinchang at 2,031m. Tanah Rata, Ringlet and Brinchang are the three main settlements in the administrative district, followed by Kampung Raja as a major centre for vegetable production. The population is approximately 35,000 people. The mean annual temperature is about 18° C, typically reaching 22–25° C by day and dropping to 9–13° C at high elevations. On Gunung Brinchang there is a radio and television station, from which a trail gives access to elfin forest.

To the south, where the Main Range is significantly narrower, but still has peaks in excess of 1,800m, Genting Highlands spreads over roughly 15km² of forest, with tourism and agriculture. The highest accessible point is Gunung Ulu Kali, at about 1,758m. There is also access from an intermediate point to Gunung Bunga Buah, which is about 1,407m high. The average temperature is about 19.7° C, and annual rainfall is 3,534mm. The access road was completed in 1969 and has been re-routed and improved since. The first hotel opened in 1971; there are now several hotels as well as the casino, a skyrail cablecar system, apartments and a theme park.

Positioned in between them is Fraser's Hill: among significant landmarks, High Pines bungalow is at around 1,315m elevation, The Gate immediately before the town is at 1,228m elevation, and the most distant trekking point at Pine Tree Hill is at about 1,524m elevation. Jeriau Waterfall provides a low point at about 1,040m. At a point where the Main Range is still moderately broad, Fraser's Hill itself is not particularly high – unlike Cameron and Genting Highlands it does not reach upper montane forest elevations – and it is situated at an east–west kink in the otherwise largely north–south-running range.

Fraser's Hill derives its name from Louis James Fraser, a Scot who began trading tin near Raub and Tranum in 1883. At the time a bullock-cart trail led from Kuala Lumpur to Raub, and The Gap (Ginting Semangkok) was a natural stopping point at the top of the pass. From The Gap, Fraser explored upwards into the mountains looking for tin, though mountains are not usually regarded as a prime source of tin ore. Nevertheless, Fraser is said to have found tin deposits, and recruited labour for a mine. A track was constructed to transport the tin ore down to The Gap, to Tranum and on to Raub, the nearest town.

Fraser died without record sometime before 1904. Various government officers such as H. N. Ridley visited over the next few years. In 1917 the Bishop of Singapore, C. J. Ferguson-Davie, trekked up from The Gap to look for Fraser's site, and reported that the place was perfect for a hill station. Work started on the access road from The Gap in 1919, and by 1922 Fraser's Hill was opened to visitors. The hill station covered 140ha of land and had over 50km of jungle paths. By 1927 there were nine bungalows for use by government officials, four houses built with the help of the Red Cross for ex-servicemen and women, three private homes, a country club, a golf course, water supply and a post office. Further bungalows were built before the Second World War.

The 1970s to the '90s saw another burst of development, including corporate bungalows, hotels and a second golf course. Faced with growing evidence of environmental impacts at Cameron Highlands, the Pahang state government in 2010 ruled out further development of virgin forest at Fraser's Hill.

The resort is situated 104km from the national capital city Kuala Lumpur and 236km from the state capital Kuantan. The winding, 8km single-track road up from The Gap was until recent times open in alternate directions each hour (odds hours for going up and even hours for going down). The drive to the top takes less than 20 minutes. The new alternative road was opened in 2001, but if for any reason one of the roads is closed, the alternating up and down timings can still be put into force.

Temperatures vary little throughout the year, rising to about 21–23° C by day and dropping to 13–17° C by night. Cloud cover is high but very variable, at 35–72 per cent, and typically greatest in November–February and lowest in July–August. Monthly mean rainfall averaged over nine years (2009–2017) was as follows (in millimetres):

Jan	Feb	Mar	Apr	May	Jun	Jul	Aug	Sep	Oct	Nov	Dec
265	228	340	352	372	221	226	284	285	361	455	342

Mean annual rainfall during the same period was 3,732mm, but this figure conceals big variations between years as well as long-term trends. Total annual rainfall over a nine-year period was as follows (in millimetres):

2009	2010	2011	2012	2013	2014	2015	2016	2017
6,692	5,214	3,808	3,422	3,308	3,383	2,519	1,925	3,319

The long-term trend is not as dramatic as these figures suggest, but still a cause for concern. The annual totals and monthly averages quoted also hide the occurrence of months when rainfall was less than 100mm – there was one such month in 2010, one in 2012, two in 2014, one in 2015 and five in 2016.

It is predicted that global average temperatures might rise 2–4° C above pre-industrial levels by the year 2100. Rises will be less in the tropics, and greater towards the poles. Even so, studies suggest that changes are already happening in the elevational ranges of various birds, insects and other animals on tropical mountains. The trends are difficult to describe because they rely on historical observations of the upper and lower limits at which each bird (or other animal species) has been seen. The highest ever or lowest ever sighting does not necessarily correspond to the average or long-term highest or lowest limits. In fact, elevational limits are always fuzzy, as populations consist of individuals that move vertically, past hills and through valleys. Upwards or downwards extensions of range are much more likely to be noticed than retreats, as the loss of a species from a given site is difficult to detect and prove. Montane forest itself reaches different limits in different places, on isolated mountains versus extensive ranges, on ridges or in gullies, so the range of different effects is multitudinous. Even the precision of height records can be questioned, whether relying on out-of-date maps or on unreliable roadside signs.

The most immediate risk at the hill stations is the loss of montane specialists. Brown Bullfinches were long known from Fraser's Hill only at High Pines Bungalow, and they have now been lost. Warming of the climate can lead to species being pushed higher and higher, confined to smaller patches around peaks, then literally being pushed off their tops. But the case of the Brown Bullfinch could equally be due to the declining health and over-maturity of the patch of introduced pines where the birds were most often seen, or to inbreeding in a very small population. A second risk is ecological pressure placed on montane species by the upwards extension in ranges of lowland birds, as has been observed from The Gap up towards Fraser's Hill. Quotation of elevation limits for each species have been minimized in this book, partly because changes continue, and because a single wandering individual may not reflect the overall norm.

Changes are real but must be assessed over longer periods and might not all be due to climate change. The forest is affected by road building that opens up habitat to invasive species, changes to agriculture, logging and other practices that might affect local weather, but also erosion, wind effects and drying. Below Genting Highlands, much forest was converted to ginger cultivation from the 1980s onwards. At Cameron Highlands, clearance for vegetable farming on the Kelantan side, the spread of farms within the settlements and increasing development all have local effects on birdlife. It should be borne in mind, however, that global change is the sum of all the local changes; attributing alterations in the bird fauna of (say) Fraser's Hill to specific local causes does not rule out a role for much more sweeping geographical changes as they are merely different aspects of the same phenomenon. Even inbreeding within small, isolated populations can be an aspect of climate change, if global warming is responsible for the fragmentation of montane birds' ranges.

The changes in birdlife recorded so far, in spite of uncertainty over elevation limits and underlying causes, are too many and too widespread to dismiss. They have been surprisingly fast across only 20–30 years, and cannot be accounted for by changes in the plant species composition of the forest, where trees may live for centuries and even understorey plants can and do live for many decades. The short-term avian changes noticed so far are more likely to be accounted for by the cumulative effects of numerous local impacts, shifts in flowering and fruiting frequency, intensity or success, and changes in insect populations.

THE FORESTS

The classic description of how forests in the Malay Peninsula differ according to elevation was given by C. F. Symington in 1943. Beginning from the coast he distinguished mangroves, freshwater swamp forest, peat-swamp forest, lowland dipterocarp forest, hill dipterocarp forest, upper hill dipterocarp forest, lower montane forest and upper montane forest. Only the last three are considered montane forest types. The transition from lowland to montane forest occurs at about 900m, which is just above the elevations of The Gap (at Fraser's Hill) and Ginting Simpah (at Genting Highlands). The transition is expressed in terms of forest structure, tree species composition, and prevalence of other ecological and taxonomic plant groups such as epiphytes and bryophytes. The relative importance of these factors, and the ways in which they are influenced by short-term weather, long-term climate, and the height and isolation of particular mountains, is complex and not always agreed upon.

The 900m transition can be thought of as typically the lowermost cloud base in Malaysia, and about 6 per cent of the total land area is above that elevation, the majority of it within the Main Range (Banjaran Titiwangsa). More commonly, the 'lifting condensation level', above which cloud formation is common, occurs at around 1,200m. Not only are the transitions blurry, but they vary from place to place, and between valleys (where lowland forest extends higher) and ridges (where montane forest extends lower).

Visually most distinct is the stunted form of upper montane forest known as elfin forest or montane ericaceous forest, with a canopy below 10m high (or sometimes much less), dominated by gnarled shrubby *Leptospermum flavescens*, conifers and rhododendrons.

The mountain flora contains species with origins from both Asian and Australasian sources, and important families include Lauraceae (laurels) and Fagaceae (oaks), in lower montane forest, and Myrtaceae (myrtles) and Ericaceae (heaths) in upper montane forest. Conifers include native *Agathis*, *Dacrydium* and *Podocarpus*, but not naturally pines, which in Peninsular Malaysia are planted. Epiphytes are characteristic, and branches, tree trunks and the forest floor are sometimes covered with ferns, mosses and liverworts, with the highest incidence in upper montane forest.

Because of steep slopes and high rainfall, landslips are common even where humans have not disturbed the vegetation, and regrowth includes bamboo, tree ferns and widespread bracken-like ferns such as *Gleichenia* and *Dicranopteris*, as well as montane specialists *Dipteris* and *Matonia*. Pitcher plants, orchids, the parasitic *Balanophora*, various delicate filmy bamboos and understorey palms, and a range of understorey Begoniaceae and Gesneriaceae are well-known components of the montane flora.

The fauna is predominantly Asian. At least for birds and moths, the montane species are often of Himalayan origin or have close relatives there. The distribution of montane birds is relatively well known compared with that of other animals, though assumptions fill the gaps along the Main Range between the three best-known areas at Ginting Highlands, Fraser's Hill and Cameron Highlands.

Birdwatching Trails at Fraser's Hill

Even within a short distance of the town centre, many characteristic montane forest birds can occur, including Chestnut-capped and Chestnut-crowned Laughingthrushes, and the Streaked Spiderhunter and Black-throated Sunbird. Others are not confined to mountains (for example the Blue Whistling Thrush), and still others are open-country birds that have reached the township from the disturbed lowlands. The main birdwatching trails that take you through forest are described below, many of them starting near the town centre.

Hemmant Trail (1,000m)

The trail is predominantly wide and level, but with one short, steep stretch of steps near the midway point. There are rope rails at some places, and a couple of shelters with seating. The trail is named after Frank Hemmant, the architect who designed the nine-hole golf course in 1920. Following the contour above the outer rim of the golf course, this trail runs through disturbed secondary forest about a century old, which has grown up since the golf course was levelled (this was done by flushing earth off the slopes into the valley).

Probably the easiest of the trails within forest, a wide variety of birdlife can be seen along it, often including laughingthrushes, and the White-throated Fantail, Mountain Nunbabbler, Mountain Leaf Warbler, Green-billed Malkoha, Silver-eared Mesia and Large Niltava. The Pygmy Cupwing and Lesser Shortwing have been recorded here.

Abu Suradi Trail (350m)

Also under the misnomer 'Lichen Trail' (there are mosses, liverworts, plenty of filmy ferns but few lichens along it), this trail begins very steeply until it levels off near the top towards Maybank Bungalow. In the undergrowth are *Rhododendron wrayi*, a species of *Molinera* with purple under surfaces to the leaves, and the fallen pink-white blossoms of *Schima*. There are conifers (*Dacrydium*) and ferns (*Osmunda* is an indicator of acid soil conditions). This was one of the first areas to be given a tin-ore mining lease at Pamar Lebah in 1899. The Grey-throated Babbler is likely to be seen here, as well as the Chestnut-capped Laughingthrush, Lesser Racket-tailed Drongo and Silver-eared Mesia.

Mager Trail (310m)

The trail, beginning near the town centre and ending near the government clinic, is wide and level, with few obstacles to impede views. It is well suited to beginners. F. W. Mager was the Public Works Department engineer who supervised earthworks for the road up from The Gap in 1918–1921, surveyed the routes of the roads within Fraser's Hill and selected sites for the first wave of bungalow construction. Along the trail there are particularly statuesque trees, in which bird waves can be seen if a mixed foraging flock passes through. Mountain Tailorbirds ('Leaftoilers') occur in thickets of ferns and wild ginger in more disturbed parts of the trail.

Bishop's Trail (1,500m)

Created as a bridle path by Bishop Ferguson-Davie of Singapore in about 1917, the trail starts below the site of his former house, 'The Retreat' (later Bishop's House, now demolished). After the initial descending stretch to a T-junction, turn right and follow the trail mostly along the contour, but with ups and downs to cross streams and gulleys. The trail has a particularly rich and lush flora, varied herbs in the understorey and some particularly fine giant strangling fig trees. After 1.5km, turn right and climb up to Muar Cottage in order to return by road.

   Bishop's Trail was the classic site of discovery of the Rusty-naped Pitta in the 1970s. Almost every resident bird can be seen here in due time, including the Golden Babbler, fulvettas and leaf warblers, Black Laughingthrush, drongos, woodpeckers, Red-headed Trogon and many others. The vagrant Eurasian Woodcock has been reported, as has the resident Mountain Peacock Pheasant. Wren Babblers prefer moist forested gullies.

Maxwell's Trail (900m)

Instead of turning right at the end of Bishop's Trail to Muar Cottage, it is possible to continue straight on along Maxwell's Trail, but the risks of getting lost are higher and warnings are sometimes in place. The trail is more slippery, often with more leeches, and with more disturbed understorey including tree falls, patches of bamboo and wild gingers. The large tree *Dipterocarpus retusus* is common, dropping fruits the size of big musket balls with two dried brown wings. The trail emerges at a steep descent to Corona nurseries (the old Labour Lines) below Pines Resort, at the head of the new descent road to The Gap.

Kindersley Trail (110m)
The trail begins near the town centre, at the start of Jalan Lady Guillemard. There is a steep, challenging but short climb at the start. The trail emerges near a rest hut on Mager Road (Selangor), between Richmond Road and the Methodist Bungalow. It is named after Richard Kindersley who, in the Federal Council in the 1920s, successfully pushed for Fraser's Hill to be made a nature sanctuary.

Pine Tree Hill Trail (over 5km)
A slog more suited to serious jungle trekkers than casual birdwatchers, the trail begins just before High Pines Bungalow at nearly the highest point in Fraser's Hill. This was the classic site for the Brown Bullfinch, now gone, but the Black-throated Sunbird, Little Pied Flycatcher and Large Niltava are frequent. Trekkers are supposed to inform the local police before setting out because there have been several cases of lost visitors, with very serious consequences. Do not go alone. Remember that you must return the same way, making this a 10km walk, in places poorly marked, with many steep stretches. Though not ideal for building up a bird list quickly, it can be delightful to sit and wait for whatever turns up. Wedge-tailed Pigeons and Malaysian Peacock Pheasants have been seen. Evocative sounds of Mountain Imperial Pigeons, cuckoo doves and green pigeons, as well as the songs of gibbons (Siamang, a large gibbon, nearby and White-handed Gibbons far downslope) can provide a wonderful experience.

Girdle Road (3km)
Also known as the Telekoms Loop, off-road parking is possible on the verge where the one-way loop road begins. As this is a motorable public road, take care to avoid traffic when walking. The road is shaded by overhanging trees in many places, open in others; there can be good views of aerial swifts and swallows, and the possibility of raptors and forest birds flying above canopy level. Distant views to the roadside trees ahead offer the chance for early detection of bulbuls, babblers, laughingthrushes, minivets, Black and Crimson Orioles, and the Lesser Shortwing and other skulkers, before they have been flushed. The Cutia, Jambu Fruit Dove, Greater and Lesser Yellow-naped Woodpeckers, and Bushy-crested Hornbill have all been seen from the roadside.

Roads in Selangor
On arrival at the top gate on the access road to Fraser's Hill, the first road to the right takes you from Pahang into Selangor. A quieter part of the hill station, this offers a few big houses with neat gardens surrounded by tall forest trees. Oriental Magpie-robins are commonly seen, as well as Black-throated Sunbirds, Streaked Spiderhunters and an array of strictly forest species that can include the Cutia and Red-headed Trogon. Turning left then takes you to a feeding station set up by photographers near Richmond Bungalow, good for the Emerald Dove, Malaysian Hill Partridge and perhaps Pygmy Cupwing; turning to the right leads to a school field, where occasional open-country migrants can be seen. Do not act suspiciously near the adjacent defence training centre.

Jeriau Waterfall Road

A road leads from near the food courts downhill past the Smokehouse to Jeriau Waterfall. Along the way was the former rubbish dump, famed for its stench, flies and hence insectivorous birds, but the dump has now gone. Taller trees might host Black-thighed Falconets, Wedge-tailed and possibly Yellow-vented Pigeons, and a range of woodpeckers. Continuing downhill, Siamang may give their fantastic chorus overhead. On the roadside are several old coppicing Southern Oaks *Trigonobalanops verticillata*, a Fraser's Hill speciality. The golf course created in the 1990s (accessed through the failed 1970s mushroom farm) has been implicated in changed wind patterns, tree falls, and sedimentation of the stream and waterfall, but has opened opportunities for Grey-rumped Treeswifts, Rufescent Prinias, Yellow-vented Bulbuls, Oriental Magpie Robins and flowerpeckers, as well as montane Silver-eared Mesias, drongos and Black-throated Sunbirds.

The Gap

A fine rest house, built around 1926, operated here till the 1990s but is now abandoned. This is a fine place to seek lowland birds at 800–900m elevation, at the upper limit of their range; many birds in this book on the Fraser's Hill list are known only here. Hill specialists could potentially include the Pin-tailed Parrotfinch, Ferruginous Partridge and White-hooded Babbler. The Bat Hawk and Malaysian Eared Nightjar may be spotted at dusk. The tall secondary growth and fringing forest are good for bulbuls, leafbirds, minivets and Everett's White-eyes. More open views permit sightings of swifts, swallows and raptors; there has been a famous nest site for Blyth's Hawk Eagle 500m back towards Kuala Kubu Bharu. Pigeons and hornbills can be seen if fruits are available, though the spectacular fig in front of the rest house fell in the 1990s.

The Old Ascent Road

Indented labour under Frank Mager created the old 8km access road, replacing the former bridle path to Fraser's Hill. Road traffic was formerly one hour up, one hour down, with gates and guards at top and bottom, and this situation can still occur if the descent road is inoperable. Traffic is much lighter on weekdays than at weekends. If it is rainy or misty at the top of Fraser's Hill, The Gap can sometimes offer better weather. An early morning session at The Gap followed by a slow walk up occupies at least half a day, with a good cross-section of elevation changes in forest and birdlife. All the lowland and hill-slope species on the list are possible. The Silver-breasted Broadbill may be seen in side gullies on the upslope side of the road. On the road itself, migrant Grey Wagtails occur in season, Slaty-backed Forktails can be seen, and the Malayan Whistling Thrush is a possibility. Progressively higher, look for shrike-babblers, sibias, minlas, Fire-tufted Barbets and other barbets, and Orange-bellied Leafbirds.

About 2km above The Gap is a forest trail leading left to a research plot. In bamboo along the trail the Bay Woodpecker, Grey and Buff Woodpeckers and Rufous-fronted Babbler may be seen, and there is a chance of hearing the Ferruginous Partridge. Marbled Wren Babblers can also occur here.

The New Descent Road

Built around 1993–1996, and fully opened in 2001 to relieve the one-way traffic scheme, the new descent road initially incurred repeated landslips and was closed for long periods. Now much more stable, it provides wider landscape views than the old ascent road, with more open roadside vegetation, where Stripe-throated Bulbuls, Rufescent Prinias and Barred Cuckoo Doves may be seen. Hornbills and raptors may be viewed at a distance, as well as barbets, bulbuls and pigeons feeding in trees, forest-edge flycatchers such as Asian Brown and Verditer Flycatchers, and Blue-throated Bee-eaters on exposed perches.

THE BIRDS

Birds are at the mercy of the birdwatcher, and ethical behaviour is necessary when watching, photographing and recording birds. Every birdwatcher should know the value of being quiet, wearing clothing of subdued colours and not disturbing birds at the nest. Along the roads and trails at Fraser's Hill, birdwatchers and photographers have set up various feeding spots to attract birds in to view them. This should not be done too often, should not involve unsuitable foods and should not block traffic or the enjoyment of the trails by others. There have been reports of large crowds gathering at such spots, to the displeasure of other visitors to the hill. Likewise, the use of playback of recorded calls and songs to attract birds must be done ethically, and very loud playback is counter-productive. It can lead to the abandonment of territories and breeding attempts by birds.

Both the Pahang and Selangor sectors of Fraser's Hill are protected areas, so adherence to the law (including the Protection of Wildlife Act 2010) is required. This will help bird life. So will the submission of interesting records, findings and photographs to bodies such as the Bird Conservation Council of the Malaysian Nature Society.

Strange (2004) listed 247 bird species from Fraser's Hill, but another 36 known only through nocturnal mist netting, and another 24 lowland species questionably reported only from The Gap. Most of these have now been confirmed, so the full list is about 310 species ever recorded. With the cessation of netting in the early 1970s, it will be challenging to ever again record some of the nocturnal migrants and vagrants.

The bird list includes the following main components:

1. Species confined or largely confined to montane forest above about 900m. A few are endemic to the Malay Peninsula (Malaysian Hill Partridge, Mountain Peacock Pheasant, Malayan Whistling Thrush), but many are the southernmost populations of species with a mainly Himalayan or mainland Asian distribution (e.g. Cutia and Blue-winged Minla), or further extend into Sumatra (e.g. Red-headed Trogon, Long-tailed Sibia, Fire-tufted Barbet, Black-browed Barbet, Silver-breasted Broadbill, Silver-eared Mesia, Lesser Racket-tailed Drongo and Golden Babbler). Still others have a core distribution covering mountains of the main Sunda land masses – the Malay Peninsula, Sumatra, Borneo and some in Java (e.g. Black and Crimson Orioles, Cinereous Bulbul, Streaked Bulbul, Mountain Leaf Warbler and Sunda Warbler).
2. Lowland forest birds that just reach the elevation of The Gap or a little higher.

3. Hill specialists, spanning The Gap but seldom reaching the uppermost points of Fraser's Hill (e.g. White-hooded Babbler, Stripe-throated Bulbul, Ferruginous Partridge and Bay Woodpecker).

4. Open-country generalists that have reached Fraser's Hill or its environs and make use of man-made habitats (e.g. Oriental Magpie Robin, Eurasian Tree Sparrow and Yellow-vented Bulbul).

5. Aerial feeders such as swifts and swallows that may or may not be resident and may take little account of the vegetation below them, except in so far as it provides a source of the insects flying above.

6. Migrants passing through, often not montane, and sometimes from wildly different environments (e.g. Tufted Duck, von Schrenk's Bittern, Masked Finfoot and Oriental Reed Warbler).

Special features of Fraser's Hill include its position at an east–west kink in the otherwise predominantly north–south mountain range, and its moderate elevation, both of which may encourage migratory birds to use it as a crossing point. Fraser's Hill is just too low for a few montane forest birds, such as the Bar-throated (formerly Chestnut-winged) Minla, Rufous-bellied Niltava and Tawny-breasted Parrotfinch. It is extremely marginal for the Brown Bullfinch, now lost, whose past presence at Fraser's Hill might only have been due to artificially planted pine trees, somewhat resembling its Himalayan forest habitat. Fraser's Hill also lacks one or two birds found on isolated mountains elsewhere in the Malay Peninsula: the Hill Prinia *Prinia atrogularis*, the Crested Argus *Rheinardia ocellata*, and the distinctive race of Grey-headed Woodpecker that occurs on Gunung Tahan (the peninsula's highest mountain) and at Cameron Highlands.

Although Fraser's Hill lacks the scenic and ecologically interesting elfin form of upper montane forest, there is no other site in Malaysia that offers such a convenient and easily walked transect from lowland forest to mountain peaks. As noted earlier, this partly accounts for the poor comparability of bird lists from Cameron and Genting Highlands. Furthermore, parts of Fraser's Hill deserve more attention (forest along the new descent road, and forest along the Pine Tree Hill trail, but with due care and attention to personal safety), as well as the road descending from The Gap down through lowlands towards Tranum and Raub.

Fraser's Hill is excellent for making observations of, for example, the composition and behaviour of birds (and mammals) in mixed foraging flocks, records of diet, and in principle observations of the effects of climate change. Lee et al. (2005) examined the effects of local-scale habitat disturbance on mixed species flocks along an escalating gradient of man-made changes in a submontane tropical rainforest in Peninsular Malaysia. They found that mixed species flocks in the forest interior and forest-edge habitats contained more species than those observed in more urban habitat. Some species were more likely than others to drop out of mixed species flocks. Birds particularly sensitive to habitat disturbance were forest corvids, sunbirds and warblers, those that had restricted elevational ranges, and those that were exclusively dependent on primary forest and understorey microhabitats. They concluded that submontane mixed species flocks, in the sort of habitat represented along the access roads to the hill stations of the Main Range, are affected by even small-scale urbanization, and that they can be used as effective ecological indicators.

Malaysian Hill Partridge ■ *Arborophila campbelli* 28cm

DESCRIPTION Round-bodied, predominantly ashy-grey; head blackish with white cheek-patch, white above bill and interrupted white brow to nape; back browner with dark barring; flanks buff with dark bars; wings crossed by several diagonal dark and pale grey bars. Bill black (with red tip in juveniles), legs bright pinkish-orange. **DISTRIBUTION** Endemic to mountains of Malay Peninsula; resident. **HABITAT AND HABITS** Found above 1,000m in upper hill dipterocarp, lower and upper montane forests, where it skulks in the undergrowth, in pairs or family parties. Usually very hard to see, it has become tame at some spots where food is provided by photographers at Fraser's Hill. Call a series of ringing couplets and single notes by the two sexes, often duetting.

Ferruginous Partridge ■ *Caloperdix oculeus* 25cm

DESCRIPTION Small partridge with bright rufous-orange on head and neck, breast and belly, and flanks and upper back barred and scalloped black and buff. Lower back scalloped black and rufous, and wings dark brown with black drop-shaped spots. Male and female similar. **DISTRIBUTION** Malay Peninsula to Sumatra and Borneo; resident. **HABITAT AND HABITS** Apparently prefers hilly terrain, occurring singly or in pairs in hill dipterocarp forest and bamboo, where it has been recorded around The Gap below Fraser's Hill. Rarely heard (or not recognized) call is an accelerating series of notes that suddenly slows and breaks up at the end into 2–3 harsh syllables. Sightings are still rarer, and distribution and ecology of this species are poorly understood.

Mountain Peacock Pheasant

■ *Polyplectron inopinatum* 45–65cm

DESCRIPTION Dark grey with rufous wings and tail, appearing bright chestnut in good light; wings with small black eye-spots; uppertail-coverts and long, tapering tail with big, lozenge-shaped, iridescent green spots. Female smaller than male, with shorter and duller tail. **DISTRIBUTION** Endemic to Peninsular Malaysia and possibly just north of border into southernmost Thailand. At all three hill stations; at Fraser's Hill sometimes along Bishop's and Pine Tree Hill trails. **HABITAT AND HABITS** Found singly or in small family groups, in moist montane forest above 800m, including tall forest and elfin forest. Usually silent, but males occasionally give a series of harsh *kek-kek* or *kek-kek-kek* notes, in clusters every few seconds. On the ground, often creeping between and beneath understorey foliage.

Spotted Dove

■ *Spilopelia chinensis* 30cm

DESCRIPTION Overall light brown with slight pinkish hue; plumage has darker upperparts; black patch with white spots across nape diagnostic; white vent; light yellow iris; red feet. **DISTRIBUTION** Not recorded at Fraser's Hill, but in agricultural areas mainly at lower elevations in Cameron Highlands. Found across India and China to SE Asia. Common resident in Malaysia and Singapore. **HABITAT AND HABITS** Inhabits open country, scrub, plantations, gardens and villages. Usually seen singly on in pairs, feeding on the ground or engaged in courtship. Takes off when disturbed at close quarters. Sometimes kept as a cage bird.

Barred Cuckoo Dove ■ *Macropygia unchall* 40cm

DESCRIPTION Slim, long-tailed pigeon, light brown on head, neck and underparts, and medium brown on back, wings and tail. Male finely barred black on breast and upperparts; female more heavily and extensively barred all over, including head, neck and underparts. **DISTRIBUTION** NE India and Himalayas, through Malay Peninsula, to Sumatra, Java, Bali and Lesser Sunda Islands; resident. **HABITAT AND HABITS** Found in forest and forest

edges, from about 800m upwards to highest peaks. Scarcer than the Little Cuckoo Dove (see below); sometimes seen in flight above forest canopy. Call is a deep *wu-wup!* repeated in a long, slow series.

Little Cuckoo Dove ■ *Macropygia ruficeps* 30cm

DESCRIPTION Beautiful highland dove with rich chestnut plumage with slightly darker tone on wings and mantle; legs red; barring on upperparts and black mottling on chest; iris white. Adult male has glossy green and lilac nape that female lacks. **DISTRIBUTION** Confined to SE Asia. Common hill and montane resident in Malaysia. Not recorded in Singapore. **HABITAT AND HABITS** Regularly encountered at hill stations such as Fraser's Hill in pairs or small flocks. Fast and powerful flier above the canopy, capable of flying great distances in search of food. Generally shy but call often betrays its presence. Call is an incessant, rapid *wup wup wup …*, about two notes per second.

Thick-billed Green Pigeon ■ *Treron curvirostra* 27cm

DESCRIPTION In both sexes, overall plumage olive-green, yellow wing-bars, light green eye-ring, thick bill with maroon at base and red legs. Adult male has maroon mantle and wing-coverts; vent cinnamon. Female has darker olive-green wing-coverts.
DISTRIBUTION India, Nepal and SE Asia. Resident in Malaysia and Singapore.
HABITAT AND HABITS Frequents mangroves, well-wooded gardens, forest edges and forest; usually seen at the canopy or middle storey. Often feeds in large parties (sometimes 50 birds simultaneously) in fruiting fig trees, at times with other frugivorous birds.

Yellow-vented Green Pigeon ■ *Treron seimundi* 32cm

DESCRIPTION Overall olive-green, with golden wash on crown and forehead; paler on throat, breast, rump and uppertail-coverts. Undertail-coverts and vent bright yellow with dark green streaks, and centre of belly pure white. Central tail feathers extended to form short, blunt point. Bill and ring of bare skin around eye bright blue. **DISTRIBUTION** Mountains of Indochina (Vietnam, Laos, Thailand) and Malay Peninsula; resident. **HABITAT AND HABITS** Seldom reported, in montane forest above 1,000m, but also reported once or twice from lowland habitat, suggesting the possibility of long-distance movements in response to fruit production. Occurs in upper storey of lower and upper montane forests.

Male

Female

Wedge-tailed Green Pigeon ▪ *Treron sphenurus* 32cm

Male

DESCRIPTION Fairly bright grassy-green on head, neck and underparts; darker olive-green back, wings and tail. Male has dark maroon patch on carpal joint of wing ('shoulder'), grey upper back and orange patch on upper breast. **DISTRIBUTION** S Asia, discontinuously through Malay Peninsula, to Sumatra, Java and Lombok; resident. **HABITAT AND HABITS** Scarce at high elevations in hill stations above about 1,400m; therefore occasionally at Fraser's Hill or higher, typically in tall trees but coming down to lower storey if figs and other small fruits are available. Usually in small groups. Call an irregular cluster of short notes leading to several more sustained, higher pitched whistles.

Female

Emerald Dove ■ *Chalcophaps indica* 25cm

DESCRIPTION Handsome dove with diagnostic emerald green wings with black primaries.
Crown greyish and underparts dull maroon. Bill red; legs greyish-pink. Male brighter than female, with whiter brow and three bold, dark and light grey bands across back and rump. **DISTRIBUTION** Resident in India, across S China, to SE Asia and Australia. Resident in Peninsular Malaysia, Singapore, Sabah and Sarawak. **HABITAT AND HABITS** Keeps to the ground in forest, forest edges, mangroves and plantations. Usually solitary, feeding on fallen seeds and grubs. Flight usually low between trees, with rapid wingbeats. Call a soft, low *tick-Whooo*, repeated monotonously. Calling birds may remain at a site for several weeks before moving on, and long-distance movements have been recorded.

Mountain Imperial Pigeon ■ *Ducula badia* 46cm

DESCRIPTION Big, sombre pigeon with light grey plumage and whitish or light grey throat; mantle, wings and tail dark brown or cinnamon; legs pink. **DISTRIBUTION** India, S China, Southeast Asia, Sumatra, Java and Borneo. Resident in Peninsular Malaysia, Sabah and Sarawak but absent from Singapore. **HABITAT AND HABITS** One of the common pigeons encountered in montane forests above 900m, where it remains in tree crowns and can be inconspicuous until it moves or calls. One or two are often seen feeding together with other frugivores at fruiting fig trees. Call is a deep, resonating *whoo-Whoomp*.

Jambu Fruit Dove ■ *Ptilinopus jambu* 27cm

DESCRIPTION Male dark grass-green on neck, back, wings and tail; face carmine-red; underparts ivory-white with pink centre of breast. Female darker green all over than male, with paler belly and dull carmine (hard to see) on face. Both sexes have bright yellow-orange bill and red legs. **DISTRIBUTION** Resident in Peninsular Malaysia, Sumatra and Borneo, moving long distances between fruit sources. Recorded at all three hill stations, during daytime at lower elevations, but netting shows that it makes nocturnal flights along and across the mountain range. **HABITAT AND HABITS** Found in primary and secondary forests from lowlands to about 1,100m, feeding in fig trees and other large trees in middle and upper storeys.

Raffles's Malkoha
■ *Rhinortha chlorophaea* 33cm

DESCRIPTION Smaller than other malkohas, to which it is similar but not closely related. Male bright cinnamon-brown with long, graduated tail, dark barred with black and tipped white; skin around eye greenish; bill light green. Female similar with light grey head and breast; tail brighter brown with each feather tipped black and white. **DISTRIBUTION** S Myanmar to Sumatra and Borneo; resident. **HABITAT AND HABITS** Found in lowland forest and secondary woodland, in middle storey, usually below 1,000m. Call comprises 3–6 soft, whining notes, in a slow, descending series. Creeps through dense foliage in search of large insects (beetles, caterpillars, katydids) perched on leaves. Typically seen in pairs, along forest edges of lower elevation approaches to any of the hill stations.

Red-billed Malkoha ■ *Phaenicophaeus javanicus* 45cm

DESCRIPTION Ashy-grey above and rich cinnamon-fawn from chin to vent, with grey flanks; long, dark grey tail with white tips. The only malkoha with an entirely red bill; small area of blue skin around eye. **DISTRIBUTION** From about 14° N in Myanmar, through Malay Peninsula, to Sumatra, Borneo and Java. Resident in Peninsular Malaysia, Sabah and Sarawak, but now locally extinct in Singapore. **HABITAT AND HABITS** Similar to other malkohas, in forest and forest edges from lowlands to about 1,200m in lower montane forest. There is little information about its diet; the means of ecological separation between different malkohas would be a useful study topic.

Black-bellied Malkoha ■ *Phaenicophaeus diardi* 38cm

DESCRIPTION Sooty-grey, blacker above with an oily green gloss on wings and tail. Lacks dark chestnut belly and vent of the **Chestnut-bellied Malkoha** *P. sumatranus*, and has a darker head and much shorter tail than the Green-billed Malkoha (see p. 24), with only a narrow white tip. Like both those species, has a light green bill and bright red skin around eye. **DISTRIBUTION** Malay Peninsula, Sumatra and Borneo; resident. **HABITAT AND HABITS** Found in lowlands and hill forest, usually below 1,200m but occasionally higher, and recorded to 1,700m elsewhere. Frequents undisturbed and lightly disturbed forests, bamboo (for example at old landslips) and forest edges along roadsides. Call, seldom heard, is a soft, two-note *pew pew*, as well as the usual soft ticking given by malkohas.

Green-billed Malkoha
■ *Phaenicophaeus tristis* 55cm

DESCRIPTION Large and grey, with very long, white-tipped tail; like the **Chestnut-bellied Malkoha** *P. sumatranus*, but with paler breast and grey (not brown) belly and vent; green bill and red skin around eye. **DISTRIBUTION** From Himalayas and NE India, through S China, south to Peninsular Malaysia, Sumatra and Kangean. Resident in northern half of Peninsular Malaysia, above about 3° N. Not known from Singapore, or Sabah or Sarawak. **HABITAT AND HABITS** Similar in habits to other malkohas, foraging for large insect prey in dense foliage around tree trunks. In Peninsular Malaysia it prefers montane forest above about 850m, although in Thailand and further northwards it occurs in a wider range of habitats down to coastal mangroves, bamboo groves, orchards and plantations.

Chestnut-breasted Malkoha ■ *Phaenicophaeus curvirostris* 45cm

DESCRIPTION Large malkoha with greyish head, rufous-brown throat and underparts all the way to vent; glossy dark green upperparts, wings and slightly more than half of long tail (remaining distal part is rufous). Prominent red eye-patch, the red colour continuing across lower mandible; yellow iris. **DISTRIBUTION** From about 15° N in Myanmar and Thailand, through Malay Peninsula, to Greater Sunda Islands; resident. **HABITAT AND HABITS** Prefers forests, forest edges, plantations and wooded gardens. Usually in pairs and generally unobtrusive.

Little Bronze Cuckoo ■ *Chrysococcyx minutillus* 16cm

DESCRIPTION Small, nearly white-faced cuckoo; male has striking red eye-ring. Crown green; back, wings and tail olive-brown with greenish-bronze tone. Face and underparts white; barred narrowly with black on face and increasingly heavily on breast and belly. **DISTRIBUTION** Widespread from mainland and island SE Asia, through New Guinea to Australia, though there are significant regional differences; resident but with some local movements. **HABITAT AND HABITS** Primarily found in lowlands, in dense forest and forest edges, or heavily overgrown rubber plantations and secondary woodland. Occurs into montane elevations and has been recorded from Fraser's Hill. Call a brief trill, or a series of several descending notes with a pause before the final note.

Banded Bay Cuckoo
■ *Cacomantis sonneratii* 22cm

DESCRIPTION Fairly small cuckoo; rufous-brown above, on crown and behind eye, with pale underparts and eyebrow strongly but finely barred blackish; light streak back from gape below eye. **DISTRIBUTION** S and SE Asia, from India to Java, Bali and the Philippines; resident. **HABITAT AND HABITS** Scarce, in middle storey of tall forest, forest edges, secondary woodland and abandoned plantations, in lowlands, but sometimes reaches elevation of The Gap. Hard to spot because of sober colouring and long periods spent motionless; more easily heard than seen. Call is a series of repeated four notes, *tu-ti, tu-ti*.

Plaintive Cuckoo
■ *Cacomantis merulinus* 20cm

DESCRIPTION Slim, fairly long-tailed cuckoo with light grey head and upper breast; brown back and wings; blackish tail with white bars on outer feathers visible in flight or more reliably when seen from below. Lower breast and belly peachy-rufous. There is a rufous-brown plumage form in females, with black mottling on back, and black-and-white barring on belly. **DISTRIBUTION** SE Asia, from Malay Peninsula, to Java, Bali, Sulawesi and the Philippines; resident. **HABITAT AND HABITS** Predominantly in lowlands, in tall secondary woodland, old plantations, forest edges and sometimes urban areas, reaching occasionally to montane elevations. Recorded from Fraser's Hill. Best known by steadily rising call, a series of three-note phrases, *phee-sa-phee*, with emphasis on the third note, ascending the scale and becoming louder. Also a descending series of 8–10 notes, quickening at the end.

Sunda Brush Cuckoo
■ *Cacomantis sepulcralis* 24cm

DESCRIPTION Minimally larger than the Plaintive Cuckoo (see above), with darker grey-brown face and crown; underparts rufous extending all the way up to throat, plain in male and usually barred with light grey in female. Tail like that of the Plaintive Cuckoo. There is a rufous-brown plumage form in females, with dark brown bars on back, and black-and-white barring on underparts. **DISTRIBUTION** SE Asia, from Malay Peninsula, to Java, Bali and the Philippines; resident. **HABITAT AND HABITS** Typically more common than the Plaintive Cuckoo in extreme lowlands, in mangroves and lowland forest, but included on Fraser's Hill list. Usually in middle to upper storeys of tall trees. Series of three-note phrases like those of the Plaintive Cuckoo but hoarser and becoming more frantic; series of descending notes longer (6–20 notes), on a single pitch rather than descending.

Drongo Cuckoo
■ *Surniculus lugubris* 24cm

DESCRIPTION Glossy black all over, with slightly forked tail-tip and inconspicuous whitish barring on vent; whitish tips to underwing-coverts may be visible as pale bar in flight. Very like drongos but slimmer, with slim, weak bill. **DISTRIBUTION** S and SE Asia, to the Philippines, Java, Bali and Sulawesi, and some islands further east; resident and migrant (migrants are sometimes distinguished as the **Fork-tailed Drongo Cuckoo** *S. dicruroides*). **HABITAT AND HABITS** Found in tall forest, secondary woodland and sometimes overgrown plantations in lowlands, to about 1,000m, rarely higher. Call is a rising series of piped notes, typically 6–7, regularly spaced, and repeated endlessly. Usually perched singly in middle or upper storey.

Bock's Hawk-cuckoo
■ *Hierococcyx bocki* 40cm

DESCRIPTION Large, with generally dull grey-brown head, mantle, wings and tail, the tail bearing 3–4 broad dark bars all of similar width. Underparts white with sparse barring on lower breast and flanks; throat and upper breast plain rufous (streaked black in juveniles); yellow eye-ring and legs. **DISTRIBUTION** Mountains of Peninsular Malaysia, Sumatra and Borneo (the latter possibly distinct); resident. Passage migrant and winter visiting populations (now identified as the distinct **Large Hawk-cuckoo** *H. sparverioides*) reach some parts of SE Asia but probably not Peninsular Malaysia. **HABITAT AND HABITS** Very secretive and keeps to forests, forest edges and wooded gardens. Usually solitary; parasitizes small passerines such as leaf-warblers. Call, sometimes a conspicuous feature of Fraser's Hill, is a series of eight to more than a dozen deliberate double notes, quickening and ascending the scale.

Sunda Cuckoo
■ *Cuculus lepidus* 30cm

DESCRIPTION Light grey head and neck, paler on throat and darker on wings and tail; white breast and belly with broad, black well-spaced bars; buff on vent below tail. In some females grey on head and upperparts is replaced by rich rufous, heavily and closely barred blackish, the underparts remaining white with well-spaced black bars. **DISTRIBUTION** Malay Peninsula, through mountains of Sumatra, Borneo, Java and Bali, to Lesser Sunda Islands; resident. **HABITAT AND HABITS** Usually above 900m in montane forest, in dense foliage in middle storey; difficult to see well. Call, fairly often heard, is a three-note *hoop, hoop-hoop* or four-note *hoop, hoop-hoop-hoop*, the first note higher than the rest and followed by a very slight pause.

Indian Cuckoo
■ *Cuculus micropterus* 32cm

DESCRIPTION Very like the Sunda Cuckoo (see above) but slightly larger. Outer tail feathers have whitish bars; tail has broad black subterminal band; vent not buff but white with black bars, like breast and belly. In female small area of upper breast is light peachy-rufous, slightly barred. **DISTRIBUTION** Mainland S, E and SE Asia, to the Philippines, Borneo, Malay Peninsula, Sumatra and Java; resident and migrant. **HABITAT AND HABITS** Found in lowland and hill forests, scarcer at higher elevations and reaching into montane forest; usually in undisturbed areas but sometimes in old plantations and secondary woodland. Call very distinctive: four notes in a regular rhythm, of which the third note is higher pitched, often transcribed as *one-more-bot-tle*.

Himalayan Cuckoo ■ *Cuculus saturatus* 32cm

DESCRIPTION Very like Sunda and Indian Cuckoos
(see opposite), but black bars on underparts are narrower
and creamy tone on vent is pale. Outer tail feathers
lack white bars, as in Sunda and differing from Indian.
Female has small area of rufous at sides of upper breast.
There is a rufous form of female; light bright rufous with
narrow black barring on upperparts and underparts.

Male

DISTRIBUTION Mainland S and E Asia, wintering
throughout SE Asian mainland and islands as far as
Java, Bali, Lesser Sunda Islands and New Guinea;
migrant in Malay Peninsula. **HABITAT AND HABITS**
As a migrant, found in more open habitats than Sunda
Cuckoo, in plantations and forest edges but not usually
within forest proper; more common in lowlands but
may reach into montane elevations. Usually silent in
its winter quarters, but its 4–5-note call might be heard.
Identification of cuckoos is very challenging, and calls
are often the most reliable guide.

Female

Grey-rumped Treeswift ■ *Hemiprocne longipennis* 22cm

DESCRIPTION Large swift often
seen perched erect on exposed
twigs, with long wing-tips crossed.
Dark green-glossed grey, paler below,
with long, forked tail, small, erect
crest above bill and, in male, dark
red ear-coverts (blackish in female).
DISTRIBUTION Malay Peninsula
throughout island SE Asia, to
Java, Bali, Lombok and Sulawesi;
resident. **HABITAT AND HABITS**
Found in lowlands and hills, usually
in small parties roosting on bare
twigs on top of the canopy or on
service wires, or in elegant circling
flight with slow wingbeats; seen
alone or with other swift and
swiftlet species. Occurs over forest
and tree plantations and orchards,
sometimes reaching montane
elevations, as at The Gap.

Whiskered Treeswift

■ *Hemiprocne comata* 16cm

DESCRIPTION Small, slim and brown, with long wings and deeply forked tail; dark brown body with two white lines on sides of head (brow and moustache), and white on innermost wing feathers. Ear-coverts between two white lines maroon in male, blackish in female. **DISTRIBUTION** From about 12° N in southernmost Myanmar, through Malay Peninsula, to Sumatra, Borneo and the Philippines; resident. **HABITAT AND HABITS** Often perched on end twigs of tree crowns, with wing-tips crossed over rump, or in flight over lowland forest and just into montane forest to about 1,100m. Makes short flights after insects, typically returning to the same perch. Nest is a tiny white cup adhering to an exposed treetop bough, built by both sexes, which alternate in bringing nest material and in incubation. Recorded on approaches to Cameron and Genting Highlands but apparently not yet at Fraser's Hill.

Silver-rumped Spinetail

■ *Rhaphidura leucopygialis* 11cm

DESCRIPTION Glossy black plumage with short, square-ended tail and broad pure white rump extending well down tail and wrapped around at sides; entirely black below. Wings most distinctive, described as shaped like a butter knife, broader towards tip and narrower near base, making this one of the more easily identified swifts when in flight. **DISTRIBUTION** Malay Peninsula, to Borneo, Sumatra and Java; resident. **HABITAT AND HABITS** Seen over forest, forest clearings and tall plantations, mainly in lowlands but reaching montane elevations; often feeds over water, and often in small parties. Thought to roost in tree hollows, presumably cavities in emergent trees above general level of the forest canopy.

White-throated Needletail ■ *Hirundapus caudacutus* 20cm

DESCRIPTION Two of the needletails (White-throated and Silver-backed, see below) have blurry whitish colouring on back, like a saddle between the wings, and pale flash on innermost secondaries. White-throated has distinct, strongly defined white throat set against dark head and breast, and small white mark on forehead. **DISTRIBUTION** Himalayas, through E and NE Asia, wintering south throughout SE Asia to Australasia; passage migrant and occasional overwintering visitor. **HABITAT AND HABITS** Forages over hill and montane forests, both high in the sky and low over vegetation, rapidly and impressively. Seen in small parties or sometimes even large flocks, most likely on passage in September–November or March–April.

Silver-backed Needletail ■ *Hirundapus cochinchinensis* 20cm

DESCRIPTION Like the White-throated Needletail (see above), with pale back, but throat merely a little paler than breast, not a sharp-edged white bib. **DISTRIBUTION** Mainland S, SE and E Asia, wintering south to Malay Peninsula, Sumatra and Java; migrant. **HABITAT AND HABITS** Seen over forest in lowlands and hills, extending to montane elevations, usually in small flocks in rapid flight with plenty of gliding. Whereas most White-backed Needletails are passing through on the way to their extensive wintering quarters in Australia, Silver-backed tends to overwinter (September–April) and does not extend beyond Java.

Brown-backed Needletail

■ *Hirundapus giganteus* 25cm

DESCRIPTION Biggest of the needletails; bulky with torpedo-shaped body; back a little paler than head, rump and wings; throat as dark as breast and belly. Seen from below, all three needletails have a white chevron extending from flanks to vent. **DISTRIBUTION** S and SE Asia, to Palawan, Borneo, Sumatra, Java and Bali; resident in Malay Peninsula. **HABITAT AND HABITS** Seen in rapid flight over the canopy of forest in lowlands and hills, extending to montane elevations; typically in small flocks. If needletails pass reasonably close, a whistling of the air can be heard as they fly by. Thought to nest in cavities in tall emergent forest trees.

Plume-toed Swiftlet ■ *Collocalia affinis* 10cm

DESCRIPTION Smaller than the House Swift (see p. 35), and overall glossy blue-black; greyish chin and dirty whitish belly without clearly defined margins; tail slightly notched. Distinguished from other swiftlets in flight by small size and habit of flying very close to

the surface of vegetation such as tree crowns. **DISTRIBUTION** From Myanmar, through SE Asia, to SW Pacific. Resident from extreme lowlands to highlands in Peninsular Malaysia, Sabah and Sarawak; formerly resident in Singapore but now apparently only a visitor. **HABITAT AND HABITS** Often seen in flight over forests, forest edges, open country, towns and cities in small flocks. Occasionally skims over rivers or pools to drink. Nests in cave mouths, under eaves, tunnels and similar structures where light penetrates.

Waterfall Swiftlet ■ *Hydrochous gigas* 16cm

DESCRIPTION Equally dark above and below, without any pale markings. One of the larger swiftlets, noticeably bigger than the Edible-nest Swiftlet (see below), **Himalayan Swiftlet** *Aerodramus brevirostris* or Plume-toed Swiftlet (see opposite), about the size of a House Swift (see p. 35) with rather long, cigar-shaped body, wings broader at bases than those of other swiftlets; tail seen to be slightly notched at tip when spread to steer. **DISTRIBUTION** Peninsular Malaysia, Sumatra, Java and Borneo; resident. **HABITAT AND HABITS** Focused near waterfalls, and nests behind water flow in spray zone; therefore confined to hills and montane elevations where such waterfalls occur, and more likely at Cameron Highlands than at Fraser's Hill. Any sightings in coastal lowlands require careful verification. Small to large parties appear in rapid flight over the forest canopy.

Edible-nest Swiftlet ■ *Aerodramus germani* 12cm

DESCRIPTION Dark blackish-brown above and paler below, with slightly pale and poorly defined rump-patch sometimes visible; tail slightly notched. Nest is a good identification point, grubby white in this species, compared with dirty dark in the **Black-nest Swiftlet** *A. maximus*, and made of mosses, fibres and other scraps in the Plume-toed Swiftlet (see opposite). **DISTRIBUTION** SE Asia, from Malay Peninsula, to Sumatra, Borneo, Java, Bali and Lesser Sunda Islands, to Timor; resident. **HABITAT AND HABITS** Flies over the forest canopy, agricultural land and gardens, and occurs in towns. Nests in dark spaces such as interiors of abandoned buildings, and increasingly in the many custom-built swiftlet farms, tall blocks with numerous tiny entrances, and beams and nesting surfaces provided in darkness. Domestication has led to mixing of the gene pool from many areas, though no swiftlet farms have been permitted in Fraser's Hill.

Asian Palm Swift ■ *Cypsiurus balasiensis* 13cm

DESCRIPTION Slim, with narrow, pointed wings, dark grey-brown above and slightly paler below and on rump. Tail rather long, slender, often held compactly as a single point but revealed as deeply forked when the bird steers. Good identification point is its sweeping upwards flight to land within the leafy crowns of tree-palms. **DISTRIBUTION** Mainland S and SE Asia, through region to Sulawesi, Java and Bali; resident. **HABITAT AND HABITS** Seen over tree plantations, orchards, gardens, parks and villages, where there are tall, fan-leafed palms available for nesting. Nest is a fluffy white pad adhering to the under-surface of a hanging leaf, or alternatively within palm-thatched roofs of village houses. Rapid, direct flight interrupted by skittering changes of direction.

Fork-tailed Swift
■ *Apus pacificus* 18cm

DESCRIPTION Substantial body distinctly larger than House Swift's (see opposite), blackish-brown above and below, with sharply defined white throat, squarish white rump, and pale tips to many feathers of underparts giving scaly appearance. Tail more forked than House Swift's. **DISTRIBUTION** N and E Asia, wintering south through to whole of SE Asia to Australasia; in the region, a passage migrant and winter visitor. **HABITAT AND HABITS** Occurs over open country, cultivated land and villages in rural areas, from sea coasts to mountains; can occur anywhere but more typically seen in lowlands. Numbers vary widely, from singletons to large flocks, especially on passage, seen from September to April or May.

House Swift ■ *Apus nipalensis* 15cm

DESCRIPTION Generally medium sized with glossy black plumage and prominent white rump; throat white; tail slightly notched. **DISTRIBUTION** India and S China, to SE Asia and Greater Sunda Islands; resident. Populations from Africa, S Europe and SW Asia now split as the **Little Swift** A. *affinis*. **HABITAT AND HABITS** Prefers open country, forest edges, towns and cities. Often forms large breeding colonies under eaves of man-made structures such as buildings or bridges, cliffs or cave mouths, but such sites are scanty at the hill stations of the Main Range. Gregarious in nature, and can be very noisy at dusk when returning to roost. Look for nests or occasional birds at small towns such as Ringlet.

Blyth's Frogmouth ■ *Batrachostomus affinis* 22cm

DESCRIPTION Male has grizzled grey-brown upperparts, with fine dark bars and white spots on scapulars, finely barred whitish underparts with white speckles on brown breast, and narrow white collar. Female has rich rufous upperparts and underparts, with prominent white spots on scapulars and breast. **DISTRIBUTION** Mainland and island SE Asia, including Malay Peninsula, N Sumatra and Borneo; resident. **HABITAT AND HABITS** Found in lowlands, hills and montane elevations to about 1,700m, in undisturbed and lightly disturbed forests. Hunts for insects in low flight within forest, not above the trees, but most likely to be detected by sound. Male gives a short, soft growl, or an inflected single whistle lasting less than a second. Female gives a series of short growls lasting less than a second, or a single short, soft bark.

Malaysian Eared Nightjar ■ *Lyncornis temminckii* 27cm

DESCRIPTION Dark mottled grey and brown, with narrow white collar on breast (becoming buffy behind nape); crown feathers slightly elongated to form 'ears'. Wings and tail plain barred, without white patches. **DISTRIBUTION** Malay Peninsula, Sumatra and Borneo, and some of the intervening small islands; resident. **HABITAT AND HABITS** Most usually detected at dusk, when it calls loudly with an exhilarating three-note whistle, *tep-ti-bau!* in flight over the forest canopy. Occasionally flushed from daytime roosts on the forest floor, sometimes almost from underfoot in the leaf litter. Mostly in lowlands and hills, to about the elevation of The Gap at Fraser's Hill.

Grey Nightjar ■ *Caprimulgus jotaka* 30cm

DESCRIPTION Finely mottled brown and grey with brighter brown spots on wing-coverts; narrow white moustache stripe and white patch on either side of throat, but otherwise lacking contrast on crown and face. Pale patches near wing-tips and on outer

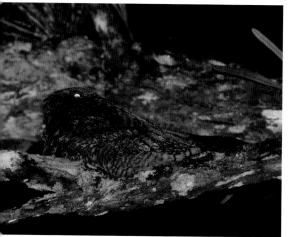

tail-tips, white in male and buff in female, visible in flight. **DISTRIBUTION** NE, SE and E Asia, migrating south to Malay Peninsula, Sumatra, Java and Borneo; migrant in region. **HABITAT AND HABITS** Found in lowlands and hills, into montane elevations such as Fraser's Hill. Frequently heard calling in its winter quarters, a quickly delivered series of *tok* notes, lasting under two seconds. If spotted in forest, it may be sitting lengthways along a large bough in the middle storey.

White-breasted Waterhen ■ *Amaurornis phoenicurus* 33cm

DESCRIPTION White face and breast, merging to rufous beneath tail, and dark back and wings make this species unmistakable. Sexes alike. **DISTRIBUTION** India, S China and SE Asia. Resident in region, as well as winter visitor and/ or passage migrant from populations further north. **HABITAT AND HABITS** Commonly seen in rank vegetation and overgrown drains, and along roadsides in rural areas, sometimes flying up when disturbed. Adults may be accompanied by several half-grown, fluffy black chicks, the pale breast plumage gradually appearing as they grow. Utters monotonous single piping note endlessly repeated, or a chorus of grating and gurgling notes in which male and female participate, competing with neighbouring pairs.

Barred Buttonquail ■ *Turnix suscitator* 16cm

DESCRIPTION Small, round-bodied, quail-like bird, variegated brown with rufous-ochre centre of belly to vent; wing-coverts, head, neck and breast scalloped black and buffy-white. Female has all markings bolder than male, and black throat and upper breast. Staring pale eye and ivory-coloured bill and legs. **DISTRIBUTION** S, SE and E Asia, to Malay Peninsula, Sumatra, Java and the Philippines; resident but making local movements. **HABITAT AND HABITS** Fairly common but hard to see in dry grassland, scrub, secondary growth in lowlands; recorded at lower elevations in agricultural land towards Cameron Highlands but not at other hill stations. Usually in pairs in which female is dominant.

Purple Heron ■ *Ardea purpurea* 80–90cm

DESCRIPTION Almost the same size as the **Grey Heron** *A. cinerea*, but slimmer. Plumage ashy-grey at base of neck, upperbody and wings. Head and neck rufous with black stripe from base of gape down to belly. Cap black. Bill yellow with some black on upper mandible; feet light yellow. In flight, separated from Grey by dark plumage, chestnut underwings and skinny appearance. **DISTRIBUTION** Africa, Europe and Asia to Sunda Islands. Resident and migrant in Peninsular Malaysia and Singapore; only known so far as resident in Sabah and Sarawak. **HABITAT AND HABITS** Associated with brackish and freshwater wetlands. Mainly solitary, often hunting quietly for fish in shallow waters by stalking and stabbing. Breeding colonies occur in lowlands, sometimes in trees with other herons and egrets, but often nests in thick vegetation on the ground. Known from Cameron Highlands, where there are freshwater bodies such as Ringlet Reservoir, but not from Fraser's Hill.

Little Egret ■ *Egretta garzetta* 55–65cm

DESCRIPTION Slim, graceful, very active egret, slightly larger but markedly thinner necked than the stocky **Cattle Egret** *Bubulcus ibis*. Non-breeding birds sport slender black bill, legs and feet, and yellowish lores. Breeding birds develop head, back and breast plumes. At all seasons, look for contrast between dark legs and yellow toes. **DISTRIBUTION** Africa, Europe, Asia and Australia. Mainly passage migrant and winter visitor to Malaysia and Singapore, but scattered records of breeding in Peninsular Malaysia and Sabah. **HABITAT AND HABITS** Mixes with other white egrets, mainly **Great** and **Intermediate Egrets** *Ardea alba* and *Mesophoyx intermedia*, in both natural and man-made

wetlands. Habits are similar to those of other white egrets but more actively chases food items and stirs shallow water with one foot to disturb prey into movement. Known from freshwater habitats in agricultural land in vicinity of Cameron Highlands, but not from Fraser's Hill.

Chinese Pond Heron ■ *Ardeola bacchus* 45–52cm

DESCRIPTION Non-breeding birds have light brown upperparts and wing-coverts; brown streaks from head to chest, and white underparts and wings; bill blackish with some yellow on lower mandible; legs yellow. When breeding, head, throat, nape and breast turn rich chestnut; mantle black; underparts remain white; feet orange.
DISTRIBUTION Resident from India, to China and SE Asia. Common non-breeding visitor to Peninsular Malaysia and Singapore; less common in Sabah and Sarawak. **HABITAT AND HABITS** Non-breeding birds encountered in small numbers in a variety of wetlands from coastal mangroves to former tin-mining pools, often solitarily or in loose associations. Before spring migration, some individuals assume full or partial breeding plumage. Known from freshwater habitats in agricultural land in vicinity of Cameron Highlands, but not from Fraser's Hill.

Striated Heron ■ *Butorides striatus* 45cm

DESCRIPTION The most common small heron, slaty-grey with dark crown, pale face markings and pale fringes to wing feathers. Juveniles brownish, spotted above and heavily streaked below. Bill dark, and legs vary from greenish to yellow or bright orange, depending on age and breeding status. Much plumage variation between individuals based on sex and geographical origins.
DISTRIBUTION Through much of tropics and subtropics in South America, Africa and Australasia, in Asia extending as far north as Japan and Ussuriland. Common throughout SE Asia as resident and migrant. **HABITAT AND HABITS** Usually seen singly, quite often in flight but usually stalking or standing on mud at edges of rivers, mangroves or the sea, or even along small forest streams. Small fish, crabs and other invertebrates are the main foods.

Oriental Honey-buzzard
■ *Pernis ptilorhyncus* 48–65cm

DESCRIPTION Medium-large raptor with variable individual plumages. In flight, longish, proportionately small, chicken-like head and long, square-cut tail with 2–3 dark bands, and long wings with numerous dark bands on under surface. Upperparts brown to chocolate or blackish; underparts cinnamon to white with highly variable amount of streaks and barring, and faint to very distinct throat gorget. **DISTRIBUTION** Temperate NE Asia, from Siberia to Japan, China and India, migrating to S China and SE Asia as far south as Java and Lesser Sunda Islands; passage migrant and winter visitor. **HABITAT AND HABITS** Seen in large numbers at key migration points near coast, but wintering birds can occasionally be found anywhere in plantations and other wooded areas. Feeds on bee and wasp larvae by raiding their nests, and also reported to take small vertebrate prey. Closely related **Sunda Honey-buzzard** *Pernis ruficollis* is resident in lowlands of Malay Peninsula and could also occur at Fraser's Hill.

Black Baza ■ *Aviceda leuphotes* 32cm

DESCRIPTION Beautiful black-and-white raptor, typically seen in flight with rounded, butterfly-like wings. Black, with large white wing-patches; white below with broad black breast-band, the belly often strongly and widely barred blackish-chestnut and white **DISTRIBUTION** From India, Himalayas and Nepal, through S China to Hainan and continental SE Asia to 14° N. Migrant to SE Asia at least to Sumatra and Java, including Peninsular Malaysia and Singapore; not recorded from Sabah or Sarawak. **HABITAT AND HABITS** Small parties soar on broad, rounded wings, showing typical pied appearance. Occurs over wooded habitats of all kinds in lowland plains, over rubber and oil-palm plantations, secondary woodland and forest, flying down to take insects from foliage, and also resting in the canopy. In southern part of Peninsular Malaysia migrants arrive in last week of October, and heaviest northwards passage is late March.

Crested Serpent-eagle ■ *Spilornis cheela* 54cm

DESCRIPTION Medium-sized, generally brownish raptor. Upperparts greyish-brown; underparts lighter brown with small white spots on breast, belly and top part of shoulder. Head darker brown (almost black in some individuals). Cere, iris and feet yellow. Bill grey. Short crest (not always visible when perched). Immatures mottled brown. **DISTRIBUTION** India, S China and SE Asia, to Greater Sunda Islands. Resident in Malaysia and Singapore. **HABITAT AND HABITS** Usually solitary, and often heard or seen in various habitat types such as mangroves, forest, residential areas (with nearby forested areas) and oil-palm plantations. At times, seen perched on vantage points. Diet consists mainly of snakes and other small vertebrates.

Bat Hawk ■ *Macheiramphus alcinus* 45cm

DESCRIPTION Mainly black, with small crest, bright yellow eye, and variable amount of white on throat and upper breast marred by some black streaks. Notable for rapid flight, with powerful, deliberate strokes of its long, narrow-tipped wings. **DISTRIBUTION** Tropical Africa and Madagascar; and Malay Peninsula to Sumatra, Borneo, Sulawesi and New Guinea. Resident in Peninsular Malaysia, Sabah and Sarawak; scarce non-breeding dispersant to Singapore. **HABITAT AND HABITS** Typically seen in late afternoon and evening in forest, especially near limestone cliffs with caves, where bats emerge and are hunted; also over secondary woodland and open country. Can overhaul most bats in direct flight, or grab one from the edge of a flock, using its foot to catch the bat, then swallowing it in flight. Its big stick nests have been found a number of times, a pair using the same nest site repeatedly.

Blyth's Hawk-eagle

■ *Nisaetus alboniger* 52–58cm

DESCRIPTION Medium-sized raptor with black upperparts and prominent crest visible when perched; underparts white marked with black vertical streaks on chest, and horizontal barring on belly; tail black with broad white band; feet yellow. **DISTRIBUTION** From about 10° N through Malay Peninsula, Sumatra and Borneo. Resident in hilly areas to 1,900m in Peninsular Malaysia, Singapore, Sabah and Sarawak. **HABITAT AND HABITS** Usually seen soaring over the forest canopy, in lowlands and montane forest, or waiting on high branch in search of prey that includes lizards, bats and other small mammals. Builds large nest in a tall tree, at the point where several main boughs diverge to form tree crown and where flight access is easy. A successful nest site is used repeatedly for several years.

Changeable Hawk-eagle ■ *Nisaetus limnaeetus* 60–75cm

DESCRIPTION Medium-sized raptor with two morphs. Dark-morph individuals blackish brown in plumage with yellow feet; dark terminal band on tail visible in flight. Pale-

morph birds generally dark brown on upperparts with whitish underparts and head, marked with streaks on chest and belly. In flight, 4–5 dark bands across tail (up to seven in juveniles). Small crest at times visible when perched. **DISTRIBUTION** India, through SE Asia to Sunda Islands. Resident at low elevations in Peninsular Malaysia, Singapore, Sabah and Sarawak. **HABITAT AND HABITS** Pale morph is more commonly encountered than dark morph. Raptor of wooded country and forest (ranging from disturbed to primary forests), or of forest patches in a matrix of agriculture and settlements. Usually seen soaring over the canopy, or heard calling, a two-note or three-note *whe Wheet!*

Rufous-bellied Eagle ■ *Lophotriorchis kienerii* 45–60cm

DESCRIPTION Black crown, sides of face, crest, hindneck and back; tail dark grey with dark bars; wings dark, barred when seen in flight. Throat, sides of neck and upper breast white with fine dark streaks; lower breast to vent and thighs feathered rufous. In juveniles back and wings are less black than in adults, underside is white not rufous, and pale brow separates dark crown from dark sides of face. Spread wing is pinched in at base, giving a slightly butterfly-like outline. **DISTRIBUTION** Mainland SE Asia, to the Philippines, Java and Lesser Sunda Islands; resident throughout region including Malay Peninsula. **HABITAT AND HABITS** Scarce in undisturbed and logged forests in lowlands and especially hills, reaching elevations above The Gap at Fraser's Hill.

Black Eagle ■ *Ictinaetus malaiensis* 65–80cm

DESCRIPTION Large, very long-winged bird, in which tips of primaries extend beyond tail when perched; shows very big, broad wings in flight. Virtually black all over; tail with slightly paler bars. Juveniles dark brown with paler barring on undersides of wings and tail. **DISTRIBUTION** S, SE and E Asia, extending to Java, Bali, Sulawesi and other

Indonesian islands to east. **HABITAT AND HABITS** Typically seen soaring long distances over the forest canopy, seeking squirrels and other arboreal vertebrate prey. In Peninsular Malaysia more usually seen over montane forest, though it extends to lowlands elsewhere in the region. At Fraser's Hill, numbers have declined over the past several decades.

Crested Goshawk ■ *Lophospiza trivirgata* 30–45cm

DESCRIPTION More heavily built than sparrowhawks. Adults have dark head, and dark brown back and wings; longish tail crossed by four broad dark bars; throat white with blackish stripe down centre; upper breast broadly streaked and lower breast barred brown. Crest inconspicuous. Immatures paler overall than adults; sparsely mottled brown below. In flight, banded tail and wings, the wing-tip showing six feathers. **DISTRIBUTION** S and SE Asia, to Sumatra, Java, Bali, Borneo and the Philippines; resident. **HABITAT AND HABITS** Forest bird, in lowlands and reaching well into montane elevations, seen high overhead in thermals, over the forest canopy or perched in middle or upper storey. Prey consists of small vertebrates.

Chinese Sparrowhawk ■ *Tachyspiza soloensis* 25–30cm

DESCRIPTION Adult male largely unmarked, with smoky-grey head, wings, back and tail, the breast peachy-pink fading to white on belly. Female larger, with faint dark stripe down centre of throat, and breast deeper pink with faint barring. Eye dark red in male, yellow in female. In flight, distinctive black wing-tips, and pink of breast extends to wing linings. Tail faintly barred. **DISTRIBUTION** E Asia, migrating south to island SE Asia, Wallacea and Australasia; in Malay Peninsula migrant and on passage. **HABITAT AND HABITS** Usually in flight on migration, sometimes with other raptors, in lowlands but reaching into hills and lower montane elevations; in overgrown plantations, forest edges and occasionally undisturbed forest.

Japanese Sparrowhawk ■ *Tachyspiza gularis* 25–30cm

DESCRIPTION Adult male has dark grey head, back and wings, pale throat, and orange-rufous breast indistinctly barred towards belly. Tail dark grey with 4–5 dark bars. Adult female larger, dark grey-brown above and white barred with brown below; chin (with central stripe) and vent white. Immatures brown above, mottled brown on white below. In flight, strongly barred tail and underwing, with rounded wing-tip showing five feathers. **DISTRIBUTION** E Asia, migrating south as far as Java, Bali and Lesser Sunda Islands; in Malay Peninsula a migrant and on passage. **HABITAT AND HABITS** Usually in flight on migration, sometimes with other raptors, in lowlands but reaching into hills and lower montane elevations; in overgrown plantations and forest edges.

Oriental Bay Owl
■ *Phodilus badius* 22–28cm

DESCRIPTION Beautiful smooth, pearly-grey face and underparts, the heart-shaped face disc with rounded 'ears' and dark eyes set in slanting blackish smudges; sparsely spotted underparts. Above, rich chestnut with specks of dark and white. **DISTRIBUTION** Mainland SE Asia, to Malay Peninsula, Sumatra, Borneo and Java; resident. **HABITAT AND HABITS** In lowlands, occasionally reaching into montane elevations, in the understorey of undisturbed and lightly disturbed forests. Hunts for large insects and small mammals, clinging to vertical stems and flying or pouncing to catch prey on the leaf litter. Call is a haunting series of wails, two loud ones followed by several more, fainter, wavering up and down the scale. Recorded on approaches to Fraser's Hill.

Brown Hawk-owl ■ *Ninox scutulata* 30cm

DESCRIPTION Larger than a scops-owl, with rounded head, no ear-tufts, and round, staring yellow eyes. Plumage dark brown, including face, with some pale spotting on upperparts, and brown increasingly broken up by white on lower breast and belly; tail barred. **DISTRIBUTION** From India and Sri Lanka, throughout E Asia to Korea and Japan, through SE Asia to Sumatra, Borneo, Java, Bali and the Philippines. Of these, northern continental Asian birds are now split as *N. japonica*. Resident in Peninsular Malaysia, Singapore, Sabah and Sarawak, and migrant form also occurs throughout region. **HABITAT AND HABITS** Resident in lowland forest, forest edges and tall secondary woodland, at low altitudes. Most often detected by frequent calling, *ke-wick*. Hunts primarily for insects, and can sometimes be seen by day. Migrant form occurs at wider range of altitudes to 2,000m.

Collared Owlet ■ *Glaucidium brodiei* 16cm

DESCRIPTION Small, round-headed owl with yellow eyes, speckled crown, brown speckles and bars above and below, and whitish centre of breast and belly. On back of head are two blackish patches on a pale-speckled background, resembling eyes. **DISTRIBUTION** SE Asia to Malay Peninsula; resident. Similar species but with differing call occurs in Sumatra and Borneo. **HABITAT AND HABITS** Occurs in montane forest from 900m upwards, in middle and upper storeys, feeding on insects and perhaps small vertebrates. Known from all the hill stations. Active by day and night, calling at any time but particularly pre-dawn and post-dawn, a deliberate and clear, four-note call, *toop, te-toop toop*, given at intervals for a few to hundreds of repetitions.

Reddish Scops-owl
■ *Otus rufescens* 16cm

DESCRIPTION Dark rufous-brown crown; dark upperparts with darker and lighter speckles, paler rufous underparts spotted with black; eyes dark brown. Noticeable 'ears' above rufous buff face-disc and dark smudges around eyes. **DISTRIBUTION** Malay Peninsula, Sumatra, Borneo and W Java, in tall lowland and hill forests to about 1,100m; resident. **HABITAT AND HABITS** Found in middle and lower storeys of tall forest. Active at night in search of insects and small vertebrates on the forest floor and understorey, and occasionally disturbed from roost by day. Call a single hoot, repeated at intervals of about five seconds. Occurs to above The Gap at Fraser's Hill; not recorded at other hill stations but should occur in forest towards lower elevations.

Collared Scops-owl ■ *Otus lempiji* 21cm

DESCRIPTION Small, rufous-brown owl with short ear-tufts; back speckled, mottled and spotted darker; underparts faintly vermiculated and streaked darker. Fronts of ear-tufts, and a variable broad collar around neck, cream to deep warm buff. Grey-and-rufous plumage morphs exist. Eyes dark brown. **DISTRIBUTION** Resident from India and Sri Lanka, to Siberia and Japan, south through SE Asia to Java and Bali. Resident in Peninsular Malaysia, Singapore, Sabah and Sarawak. **HABITAT AND HABITS** Keeps to tall secondary woodland, tree plantations and well-wooded gardens, and less commonly found in undisturbed forest in lowlands, hunting for beetles, cockroaches, crickets, small lizards and other small vertebrates at night. Call is a soft *po-up*, on one pitch or deflected downwards on second note, repeated at regular intervals of about 12 seconds; from a distance it sounds like a single note. Recorded below Fraser's Hill but not other hill stations.

Brown Wood-owl
■ *Strix indranee* 45cm

DESCRIPTION Distinguished from the Barred Eagle-owl (see opposite) by rounded head with no ear-tufts and distinct rufous mask, outlined with dark surround, and darkening to smudges around dark eyes. Finely barred below, and lacks spots on crown. **DISTRIBUTION** India south of Himalayas, through S China to Taiwan, and through SE Asia to Sumatra, Borneo and Java. Resident in Peninsular Malaysia, Sabah and Sarawak; not recorded from Singapore. **HABITAT AND HABITS** Occurs in forest interiors, from extreme lowlands up through lower montane forest, rarely to about 1,700m. Sometimes comes to forest edges, but usually waits on a branch in middle storey, scanning around to look and listen for prey. Call, made around dusk and at night, is a wavering, deep *huhuhooo*.

Mountain Scops-owl ■ *Otus spilocephalus* 18cm

DESCRIPTION Rufous-brown to grey-brown plumage, finely vermiculated with black above and particularly on the underparts; pale edges to the scapulars; eyes yellow. 'Ears' are present but not conspicuous; facial disc is pale towards centre, darkening towards edges. Speckling without streaking below distinguish it from migrant **Oriental Scops-owl** *O. sunia*, and yellow eyes and greyer speckled plumage from the Reddish Scops-owl (see p. 47). **DISTRIBUTION** S, SE and E Asia, south to the Malay Peninsula, Sumatra and Borneo; resident. **HABITAT AND HABITS** In montane forest at all three hill stations, above about 900m. Usually in the understorey but hard to locate if it does not call and has apparently shown a long-term decline at Fraser's Hill. Even when calling in the lower storey, a high-pitched two-note whistle at intervals of up to 10 seconds, it is difficult to pinpoint on the perch.

Orange-breasted Trogon
■ *Harpactes oreskios* 29cm

DESCRIPTION Medium-small trogon. Olive head and upper breast, greener in male and browner in female; brown upperparts, more chestnut in male; orange-yellow lower breast. Small circle of blue skin around eye. **DISTRIBUTION** From SW China, through Myanmar and mainland SE Asia, Malay Peninsula, to Sumatra, Borneo and Java. Resident in Peninsular Malaysia, Sabah and Sarawak; not recorded from Singapore. **HABITAT AND HABITS** Found in middle and lower storeys of tall lowland and lower montane forests, from sea level to about 1,300m on mountain slopes. Call is introduced by one or two slow, separate notes, followed by series of three or four quick notes on one pitch. Insects are snatched from foliage. Like in other trogons, nests are in rotten stumps.

Red-headed Trogon ■ *Harpactes erythrocephalus* 33cm

DESCRIPTION Large trogon with diagnostic red head in male and cinnamon head in female. Both have reddish underparts with white 'crescent' on chest (sometimes hidden between feathers), cinnamon back and upper surface of tail, and black wings with whitish stripes on wing-coverts. **DISTRIBUTION** Resident from Himalaya, to S China, SE Asia and Sumatra. **HABITAT AND HABITS** Prefers hill forests above 700m; usually seen in middle storey. Generally unobtrusive; has been recorded participating in mixed foraging flocks.

Helmeted Hornbill ■ *Rhinoplax vigil* Up to 120cm

DESCRIPTION Dark grey-brown body and wings, sharply defined from white lower breast to vent; tail light grey with subterminal black band; two very long central tail feathers reaching 80–90cm (one or both may be missing). In flight the large size, long tail and white rear border to wings are obvious. In male, throat pouch, facial skin and casque are red, with front of casque and bill tip yellower. Female similar, but throat pouch and neck vary from nearly white to lurid blue-green. **DISTRIBUTION** Malay Peninsula, Sumatra and Borneo; resident. **HABITAT AND HABITS** Found in undisturbed and lightly disturbed forests, but seriously declining due to hunting on top of habitat loss; in the crowns of tall forest trees or in flight overhead. Casque-butting display flights and flight rushes through the canopy are known, and nests occur in upwards-facing tree cavities. Call a series of hoots, eventually accelerating to a wild laugh. Occurs in forest on slopes below any of the hill stations.

Great Hornbill
■ *Buceros bicornis* 90–100cm

DESCRIPTION One of the bulkiest hornbills, easily recognized by its pied appearance, with head and white parts of plumage often stained yellow by oils from preen gland. Male and female alike, except for eye colour (red in male, white in female). Casque tends to be larger in male, with black trimmings. **DISTRIBUTION** Resident in parts of India, Bangladesh and Myanmar to SW China, and south through Peninsular Malaysia to about 3° N. Absent from southern part of peninsula and Singapore, and from Borneo, but reappears in Sumatra. **HABITAT AND HABITS** Found in lowland and hill forests from sea level to about 1,300m. Typically in pairs, but sometimes gathers in larger groups at good food sources such as heavily fruiting fig trees. Call is a loud barking, the male and female alternating, either when perched or in flight.

Rhinoceros Hornbill
■ *Buceros rhinoceros* 80–90cm

DESCRIPTION Enormous black hornbill with white belly, white tail crossed by black bar, and brilliant yellow-and-red bill and casque. Male has larger casque than female, with black line on it and red eye; female has white eye surrounded by red skin. **DISTRIBUTION** Resident in suitable habitat throughout Borneo, Java, Sumatra and Peninsular Malaysia, to about 7° N in Thailand; historically in Singapore. **HABITAT AND HABITS** Found in the canopy of lowland evergreen rainforest, to 1,400m, typically in pairs and sometimes with previous young. Flocks of up to 25 occur rarely at good fruiting trees. The monogamous pair breeds without helpers, in natural tree cavities. Members of the pair advertise territory and keep in touch with a loud, nasal barking duet, *eng-gang*, often in flight.

Bushy-crested Hornbill ■ *Anorrhinus galeritus* 75cm

DESCRIPTION Dark grey-brown all over, darkest on head, paling down to wings and basal half of tail, with distal half of tail forming blackish band. Male has blue face and black bill; female has pink face and parti-coloured bill. DISTRIBUTION Resident in Borneo (Sabah, Sarawak, Brunei, Kalimantan), Natuna Besar, Sumatra and Malay Peninsula north in peninsular Thailand and Myanmar to about 14° N. HABITAT AND HABITS Found in lowland and occasionally lower montane forests, at sea level to about 1,400m or more, but most common in foothills. Noisy groups of adults and their young, giving raucous, puppy-like yelping choruses, seek a variety of fruits including some figs, and small invertebrates. Nests in tree cavity with adults helped by group members.

White-crowned Hornbill

■ *Berenicornis comatus* 80cm

DESCRIPTION Perhaps the hornbill least often seen. Distinctive shaggy white head – crown only, in female – and tail, with entirely black wings except for white trailing edge. Male also has white breast; juveniles dark all over with white-speckled head, and only distal half of tail white. DISTRIBUTION Historically, resident throughout Borneo (Sabah, Sarawak, Brunei, Kalimantan), Sumatra and Malay Peninsula north in peninsular Thailand to about 15° N, and in Myanmar to 14° N. HABITAT AND HABITS Found in lowland evergreen rainforest, from sea level to 900m, typically in small territorial groups living in lower to middle storeys. Groups usually include an adult pair with helpers and juveniles. Feeds on lizards, snakes, small birds, bats and large insects, as well as fruits but rather few figs. Call is a soft, ventriloqual cooing.

Wreathed Hornbill

■ *Rhyticeros undulatus* 80cm

DESCRIPTION Black, with entire tail white, often stained yellowish. Male has short chestnut crest, white head and neck, and yellow throat-pouch with black bar; small, ridged casque. Female has black face and neck, bluish throat-patch with back bar, and red skin around eye. **DISTRIBUTION** Found from NE India, to Malay Peninsula, Sumatra, Java and Borneo; resident. **HABITAT AND HABITS** Though largely a lowland bird, can be seen at almost any elevation, to 1,300m or higher in distant flight at any of the hill stations. Mainly a frugivore, moving in small, noisy groups. Now distinguished from **Plain-pouched Hornbill** *R. subruficollis*, which lacks black bar on pouch, migrates in huge flocks and might be seen in hill forest north of Cameron Highlands.

Fire-tufted Barbet ■ *Psilopogon pyrolophus* 28cm

DESCRIPTION Large barbet, grass-green on body and wings, with dark collar, above which

throat is yellow and ear-coverts greyish-white; crown dark, with fiery chestnut tuft above pale greenish bill that is crossed by black band. Sexes alike. **DISTRIBUTION** Resident in mountains of Sumatra and Peninsular Malaysia. **HABITAT AND HABITS** Found in canopy and middle storeys of montane evergreen rainforest, at roughly 900–2,000m, and sometimes down into the understorey along disturbed forest edges, where it feeds on many kinds of figs and other soft fruits, plus a few insects. Often located by hearing its weird rasping call, the notes accelerating to a whirr like the noise of a buzzing insect.

Gold-whiskered Barbet ▪ *Psilopogon chrysopogon* 30cm

DESCRIPTION Hefty barbet. Green with large yellow cheek-patches; front half of crown usually yellow; rest of crown red to red-flecked blue; throat and patch behind eye dull grey to brown. **DISTRIBUTION** Malay Peninsula, Sumatra and Borneo; resident. **HABITAT AND HABITS** Found in forest, forest edges and plantations, from lowlands to about 900m. Feeds on fruits especially figs, gathering with other barbets, bulbuls and pigeons. Often highly vocal, uttering a repeated couplet, *ku-took, ku-took, ku-took,* continuing for minutes on end; also a winding down series of trills. One of the barbets to be seen and heard around The Gap, and at lower elevations of Genting and Cameron Highlands.

Male

Red-throated Barbet

■ *Psilopogon mystacophanos* 23cm

DESCRIPTION Medium-sized green barbet with yellow forecrown and red hindcrown; yellow around angle of gape, and throat red with extra red spot at sides of throat/breast. In female forecrown is blue (or blue-grey) and throat plain pale green. **DISTRIBUTION** Malay Peninsula, Sumatra and Borneo; resident. **HABITAT AND HABITS** Found in forest, typically not venturing out into tree plantations, from lowlands to above 900m. Feeds on fruits, especially small figs, gathering with other barbets, bulbuls and pigeons. Vocal like other barbets, uttering a four-note *took, took-took, took,* recognizable by its slow, quick-quick slow rhythm – but with variations. May be heard at lower elevations of approaches to the hill stations.

Female

Golden-throated Barbet ■ *Psilopogon franklinii* 22cm

DESCRIPTION Green with yellow upper throat and greyish lower throat, red forehead and yellow hindcrown. Red spot on nape, and sides of head mostly grey. **DISTRIBUTION** From Nepal and NE India to S China, patchily southwards in mountains to Peninsular Malaysia; resident. **HABITAT AND HABITS** Barbet of the montane forest in the peninsula, on the Larut Range, southern part of the Main Range and scattered mountains further east. Occurs in upper montane forest above 1,400m, feeding on figs and other fruits, but the diet is not well documented. Call is a rapid, repeated *ke-triuk, ke-triuk,* and a series of trills.

Black-browed Barbet

■ *Psilopogon oorti* 20cm

DESCRIPTION Overall green with blue face, yellow crown and yellow throat, and small patches of red above base of bill, on hindcrown and sides of throat. Blue face divided by black brow, which the Golden-throated Barbet (see above) also has, and short black line at gape. **DISTRIBUTION** Mountains of Malay Peninsula and Sumatra; resident. **HABITAT AND HABITS** Found in montane forest, at about 900–1,500m, usually in the canopy feeding on figs and other fruits. Its call, two short notes and one long *tok tok trrrk,* is a characteristic sound of the forest at all the hill stations; also a winding down series of trills. Excavates or enlarges a nest-hole in soft dead wood of old tree or branch.

Yellow-crowned Barbet
■ *Psilopogon henricii* 22cm

DESCRIPTION Green, with a yellow forecrown and eyebrow, and blue hindcrown and throat; lores and narrow eye-ring black. As in most other barbets, sexes are alike. **DISTRIBUTION** From about 8° 30' N in Malay Peninsula, through Borneo and most of Sumatra. Resident in Peninsular Malaysia, Sabah and Sarawak, but never reliably recorded from Singapore. **HABITAT AND HABITS** Found in upper storey of lowland forest, from sea level to about 900m at transition to lower montane forest, where it meets but does not overlap with the Black-browed Barbet (see p. 57). Call is a repeated *tuk-tuk-tuk-tuk trrrk*, with four short notes and a long one; also a winding down series of trills. Birds gather at fruiting figs in the canopy with other barbets and frugivorous birds, but are otherwise fairly solitary.

Blue-eared Barbet
■ *Psilopogon australis* 16cm

DESCRIPTION Smallest barbet locally, all green with blue throat and hindcrown, and red face crossed by network of black lines. When calling, bare black skin-patches inflate on either side of throat. **DISTRIBUTION** Mainland SE Asia, through Malay Peninsula, to Sumatra, Borneo, Java and Bali; resident. **HABITAT AND HABITS** Found in middle and upper storeys of tall forests, from lowlands to sometimes above 1,200m, where it feeds on small figs and other fruits. Call often heard is an incessantly repeated, two-note *ketook*, sometimes seeming like a single note, given at about two calls per second. Less well known is a piercing whistle repeated once per second.

Malayan Brown Barbet ■ *Caloramphus hayii* 18cm

DESCRIPTION The most unbarbet-like of barbets, plain brown above, light brown on throat, and fading to near white breast and belly. Pale-based dark bill heavy and downcurved; feet pinkish-orange. **DISTRIBUTION** Malay Peninsula and Sumatra; resident. Now split from the **Bornean Barbet** *C. fuliginosus.* **HABITAT AND HABITS** Social, occuring in parties of 5–10 individuals that forage in the canopy but will come down to head height along forested roadsides, in search of small fruits that include figs *Macaranga* and *Homalanthera*; perhaps also insects. Members of the group chatter and buzz to one another, *tsee, tsee.*

Rufous Piculet ■ *Sasia abnormis* 9cm

DESCRIPTION Tiny, with olive crown; darker olive wings, back and tail; forehead, face and underparts rich rufous-orange. Eye red, feet yellow, and bill dark above and yellow below. Male has yellow patch on forehead above bill, lacking in female. Juveniles duller, dark olive-grey all over. **DISTRIBUTION** Malay Peninsula, Sumatra, Borneo and Java; resident. **HABITAT AND HABITS** Present in the understorey and lower levels of disturbed and undisturbed forests, in lowlands and into lower montane elevations. Very short tailed; tail is not used as a prop, and foraging occurs not on big tree trunks but on smaller saplings, bamboos, gingers and other plants. Calls include a single sharp note, or rapid series of sharp notes slightly descending; very short bouts of quick drumming have been noted. Recorded in forest below Fraser's Hill and Cameron Highlands.

Speckled Piculet
■ *Picumnus innominatus* 10cm

DESCRIPTION Very small woodpecker with olive upperparts (greyer on upper back, greener on wings and rump); conspicuous white eyebrow and white moustache streak, pale below with blackish speckles and bars. Male has yellowish patch on forehead, lacking in female. **DISTRIBUTION** From Himalayas to Borneo; resident. **HABITAT AND HABITS** Found in montane forest at about 900–1,500m, on branches and trunks of small as well as tall trees, and down to lower storey at forest edge. Usually alone or in pairs, occasionally drumming – weakly, given its size – or calling with repeated single notes, *tsik!* Found at all of the hill stations, sometimes caught up in mixed foraging flocks.

Grey-and-Buff Woodpecker ■ *Hemicircus concretus* 14cm

DESCRIPTION Small woodpecker with disproportionately big head and crest, the crest coloured brilliant scarlet in male, grey in female. Face and underparts uniform grey; back and wings blackish scalloped with white, increasing to strong white bars on secondaries. Young birds barred with buff below, scalloped with rufous above, with black-speckled rufous crown. **DISTRIBUTION** Malay Peninsula, Sumatra, Borneo and Java; resident. **HABITAT AND HABITS** Found in middle storey of tall forest of varied types, from the coast to upper hill and lower montane forests, where it forages on trunks and branches of both smaller and larger trees. Recorded from vicinity of Fraser's Hill but not as yet from the other hill stations.

Bamboo Woodpecker ■ *Gecinulus viridis* 24cm

DESCRIPTION Entirely olive-green from
face to tail, greyer on lower breast and
belly, brighter on wings. In male crown is
scarlet from forehead to nape (lacking in
female); feathers of hindcrown very slightly
elongated. In bright light, the very faintest
of brighter bars across the secondaries can be
visible. Bill short, light grey; feet greenish-
grey. **DISTRIBUTION** Limited range from
south-central Myanmar, discontinuously
through parts of Thailand, minimally
into Laos, and to mountains of Malay
Peninsula; resident. **HABITAT AND HABITS**
Characteristic of bamboo, in forest and
regrowth over old landslips, where it forages
on smaller trees and on bamboo culms; at
middle elevations in hill and lower montane
forests. Recorded from Fraser's Hill and
Genting Highlands.

Rufous Woodpecker
■ *Micropternus brachyurus* 25cm

DESCRIPTION Plumage overall rufous-
brown, slightly darker on head and tail,
with black bars on back, wings and tail.
No significant crest. Male has patch of red
below eye, absent in female, but it is not
very conspicuous against generally brown
colour. **DISTRIBUTION** From Himalayan
foothills, E India and Sri Lanka, through S
China to Hainan, south through Indochina
to Malay Peninsula, Sumatra, Borneo and
Java. Resident in Peninsular Malaysia,
Singapore, Sabah and Sarawak. **HABITAT
AND HABITS** Found in lowland forest, from
sea level to about 1,000m, where it may just
enter lower montane forest; and down into
mangroves and tall secondary forest. Usually
in tree crowns, coming lower at forest edges
and in clearings.

Buff-rumped Woodpecker ■ *Meigyptes tristis* 18cm

DESCRIPTION Small woodpecker, finely barred black and buffy-white all over, with bars whiter and broader on wings; rump buffy-white; short, triangular crest finely barred in same colour as rest of plumage. Male has a dab of a red moustache, lacking in female. Juveniles similar, but darker below and with broader barring above. **DISTRIBUTION** Malay Peninsula, Sumatra, Borneo and Java; resident. **HABITAT AND HABITS** Lowland bird just reaching into lower montane elevations, in hill forest, where it occurs mostly in middle and upper storeys but occasionally moves down to low levels, sometimes in mixed foraging flocks. Short, loud bursts of drumming, and a rapid trill. Recorded from approaches to Fraser's Hill and Genting Highlands.

Buff-necked Woodpecker
■ *Meiglyptes tukki* 21cm

DESCRIPTION Dark brown all over, with narrow buff bars on back, wings and tail; rump the same colour as back; no crest, but a broad buff band on each side of neck. Male has a dab of a red moustache, lacking in female. Juveniles similar, but with broader barring above. **DISTRIBUTION** Malay Peninsula, Sumatra and Borneo; resident. **HABITAT AND HABITS** Lowland bird just reaching into lower montane elevations, in hill forest, where it occurs mostly in middle and lower storeys, in pairs or in small family parties. Short, loud bursts of drumming, delivered more rapidly than by the Buff-rumped Woodpecker (see above), and a high-pitched trill more sustained than by Buff-rumped. Recorded from approaches to Fraser's Hill.

Banded Woodpecker
■ *Chrysophlegma mineaceum* 26cm

DESCRIPTION One of several yellow-crested woodpeckers. Rufous head and throat diagnostic, merging into barred green back and irregularly buff-and-brown banded breast and belly. Rump yellow, wings crimson. In female sides of face are duller with more white speckles than in male. **DISTRIBUTION** Resident in Java, Sumatra, Nias, Borneo, Bangka and Belitung, Singapore and Peninsular Malaysia, to about 13° N in peninsular Thailand. **HABITAT AND HABITS** Loud, repeated scream, *kwee, kwee*, may draw attention to this woodpecker of the middle storey, in tall secondary forest, parks, gardens and forest edges, to about 1,200m altitude.

Chequer-throated Woodpecker
■ *Chrysophlegma mentale* 28cm

DESCRIPTION Another yellow-crested woodpecker but set apart by greenish crown and broad zone of light chestnut from behind eye down neck and round under throat, which is chequered black and white. In female, chestnut continues as malar stripe. **DISTRIBUTION** Resident in southernmost Myanmar and peninsular Thailand, Peninsular Malaysia, Sumatra, Bangka, Java and Borneo; now lost from Singapore. **HABITAT AND HABITS** Found in lowland and hill evergreen rainforests to about 1,200m, in middle storey, foraging on trunks and larger boughs, but scarcer than either Crimson-winged or Banded Woodpeckers (see pp. 64 and above). Calls of Chequer-throated have an upwards inflection, *kiyee*, compared with all those of Crimson-winged, which have a downwards inflection.

Greater Yellow-naped Woodpecker ■ *Chrysophlegma flavinucha* 33cm

DESCRIPTION Adult dull olive-green above, lighter greenish-grey below. Triangular crest tipped bright yellow, as in Chequer-throated and Crimson-winged Woodpeckers (see pp. 63 and below), in line running down nape and neck; primaries banded black and brown. Male has yellow moustache stripe, in female inconspicuous light rufous. **DISTRIBUTION** From Himalayas discontinuously through Peninsular Malaysia to Sumatra; resident. **HABITAT AND HABITS** Fairly common, large woodpecker in montane forest from about 900m to 1,500m. In middle storey, often near quiet roadsides. Call a spaced *chup; chup; chrr*; also a single soft screech, *kwee*, which may be repeated in a wittering series. Only occasionally drums.

Crimson-winged Woodpecker
■ *Picus puniceus* 26cm

DESCRIPTION Like the Banded Woodpecker (see p. 63), but with sides of head and throat green (red moustache streak present in male); breast plain green with barring lower on belly; plain green back, yellow rump and bright crimson wings. Contrast between red crown and green face is a useful feature for identification. **DISTRIBUTION** Resident in Java, Sumatra, Nias, Borneo and Peninsular Malaysia, north to about 13° N in peninsular Thailand. **HABITAT AND HABITS** More characteristic of primary lowland evergreen rainforest than Banded, but also occurs in rubber and oil-palm plantations and secondary woodland. Characteristic call is a two-note wail, *kee-bee*, the second note lower, but it has several other types of call, each presumably with different function. Known to drum briefly and weakly.

Lesser Yellow-naped Woodpecker ■ *Picus chlorolophus* 27cm

DESCRIPTION Similar to the Greater Yellow-naped Woodpecker (see opposite), having green back and wings, olive underparts and triangular crest tipped with yellow, but smaller, with flanks narrowly barred buff, narrow whitish moustache (present in female as well as male, and outlined in red in male), rather than broad yellow one, and distinct red eyebrow or rear crown. **DISTRIBUTION** S, SE and E Asia, reaching Malay Peninsula and Sumatra; resident. **HABITAT AND HABITS** Found in upper hill dipterocarp and lower montane forests; Greater has a similar lower limit but ranges higher to upper montane elevations. Utters a series of 8–10 loud notes descending in pitch, and a single yap. Sometimes seen in mixed foraging flocks, or singly or in pairs in lower and middle storeys, it is one of the most commonly seen woodpeckers at Fraser's Hill.

Maroon Woodpecker
■ *Blythipicus rubiginosus* 22cm

DESCRIPTION Very dark-looking woodpecker, sometimes appearing almost black, with ivory-yellow bill; in good light revealed as rich plain maroon-brown, with brighter maroon on wings and tail; darker below. Reddish eye; male has inconspicuous area of red on neck below nape. **DISTRIBUTION** Sunda subregion from peninsular Thailand to Sumatra and Borneo; resident. **HABITAT AND HABITS** Wide altitudinal range, from extreme lowlands to about 1,800m in montane forest, typically in undisturbed forest but also in areas of bamboo (for instance on old landslips on hillsides), in lower and middle storeys, singly or sometimes in pairs. Call a repetitive squeak when foraging, and a high-pitched, descending trill of about six notes. Known to drum in a short burst.

Bay Woodpecker
■ *Blythipicus pyrrhotis* 23cm

DESCRIPTION Dark, like the Maroon Woodpecker (see p. 65), but face greyer and back, wings and tail rufous-brown, strongly and broadly barred with black. Underparts dark grey. Eye red; bill conspicuous yellow; male has red wrap-around patch on nape, not seen in female. Juveniles have paler head and breast, slightly speckled, and brown barring on back is more profuse, regular and paler. **DISTRIBUTION** From C Himalayas to S China and Indochina, south to Malay Peninsula; resident. **HABITAT AND HABITS** Scarce in hill forest from foothills to about 1,800m, in tall lower and upper montane forests including Fraser's Hill and the other hill stations. Keeps to middle and lower storeys, on trunks of smaller trees and on branches, and gives very short bursts of extremely rapid drumming and short but slow, few-note trills.

Orange-backed Woodpecker ■ *Reinwardtipicus validus* 30cm

DESCRIPTION Dark brown to black. Male brighter than female, with red underparts; female brown below; broad white band on back down to rump, becoming yellow to orange on rump; wings black, widely banded with rufous-brown. **DISTRIBUTION** Malay Peninsula, Sumatra and Borneo; resident. **HABITAT AND HABITS** Rather athletic, rangy-looking woodpecker travelling in small parties through middle storey of the forest, foraging on trunks and large boughs of big trees. Occurs from lowlands to well up mountain slopes into montane forest, where it is less common. Very brief drumming, and a variety of calls within the group, including a descending trill that fades away.

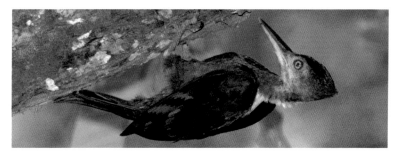

Grey-capped Woodpecker
■ *Jungipicus canicapillus* 15cm

DESCRIPTION Small woodpecker with buff underparts narrowly streaked with black; black wings, back and tail, with white barring most visible on back. Crown dark grey (with red flash in male), and face white with two broad grey bands. **DISTRIBUTION** Malay Peninsula, Sumatra and Borneo; resident. **HABITAT AND HABITS** Found in forest and plantations, mostly in lowlands but extending inland to montane elevations. More visible in treetops when viewed from slopes looking over the forest canopy, than when sought looking up from below. Produces short, very rapid drumming, and a variety of squeaking calls. Recorded at Fraser's Hill and Cameron Highlands.

Oriental Dwarf Kingfisher ■ *Ceyx rufidorsa* 13cm

DESCRIPTION Tiny forest kingfisher with brilliant orange-red bill and feet, rufous head, back and wings, and yellow breast; white patch behind ear-coverts. This is part of a complex ranging to birds with black mantle and deep blue wing-coverts, and deep blue patches on forehead and ear-coverts (known as the **Black-backed Dwarf Kingfisher** C. *erithaca*). Intermediates occur, but the two forms seem to be distinct species, Black-backed being a migrant. **DISTRIBUTION** Rufous-backed occurs from Malay Peninsula, to Sumatra, Borneo and Java, the Philippines and Lesser Sundas; resident in Peninsular Malaysia. **HABITAT AND HABITS** Found in lower storey of lowland forest, forest edges and mangroves, but also reaches montane elevations. Feeds at and near forest streams on insects and worms. Both forms (or species) can occur at Fraser's Hill and Cameron Highlands, and migrants have been netted.

Banded Kingfisher
■ *Lacedo pulchella* 20cm

DESCRIPTION Male brilliant blue on head, back, wings and tail, banded with black; underparts white, tinged with rufous on breast; deep rufous forehead, sides of face and collar. Female rufous-brown on head and upperparts, white on underparts, everywhere banded with black. In both sexes head appears shaggy and bright red bill is proportionately large. **DISTRIBUTION** Malay Peninsula, Sumatra, Borneo and Java; resident. **HABITAT AND HABITS** Found in middle storey of undisturbed and lightly disturbed forests, in lowlands but occasionally well up into montane forest, and recorded at both Fraser's Hill and Cameron Highlands. Call is a series of slow double whistles, initially with emphasis on first note of each couplet, and gradually shifting to second note of each couplet towards end.

White-throated Kingfisher
■ *Halcyon smyrnensis* 28cm

DESCRIPTION Brown throat and belly; white throat and upper breast resemble a bib; iridescent blue back and tail; red bill and feet; black upperwing-coverts. **DISTRIBUTION** Widespread from Middle East, through India, China and SE Asia. The most common resident kingfisher in Peninsular Malaysia and Singapore. **HABITAT AND HABITS** Found in a wide range of habitats near human habitation, such as mangroves, agricultural areas, plantations, gardens and urban areas. Often seen singly on exposed perches, with its calls announcing its presence. Diet varied, ranging from insects to amphibians. Present at lower elevations in agricultural land on approaches to Cameron Highlands, but not at Fraser's Hill.

Rufous-collared Kingfisher

■ *Actenoides concretus* 24cm

DESCRIPTION Forest kingfisher with greenish crown, bold black stripe through eye, blue-black moustache and entirely rufous-buff underparts. Male brighter than female overall, with glossy blue back and wings; in female upperparts are dull green with buff speckles on wings. **DISTRIBUTION** From about 11° 30' N in Myanmar and Thailand, through Malay Peninsula, to Borneo and Sumatra. Resident in Peninsular Malaysia, Sabah and Sarawak. Formerly resident in Singapore; now locally extinct. **HABITAT AND HABITS** Found in middle and especially lower storeys of lowland forest, from sea level to about 1,200m in lower montane forest, where it perches motionless until it spots an insect, small lizard or snake. Usual call is a wavering, upwards whistle, delivered in a long series.

Red-bearded Bee-eater

■ *Nyctyornis amictus* 33cm

DESCRIPTION Overall emerald or grass-green, heavy-headed bird with red throat and breast, giving it an appearance of a 'beard'; lilac crown, orange-red iris and grey feet. Bill black, slender and strongly curved. **DISTRIBUTION** From Myanmar to Sumatra and Borneo, from lowlands to about 1,100m; resident. **HABITAT AND HABITS** Typically found in the forest or its edge on a perch, in middle to upper storeys, which it uses in sallying in pursuit of insects such as bees, wasps, termites and butterflies; also known to take small vertebrates such as arboreal lizards. Usually solitary or in pairs. Excavates burrows in banks of streams to nest. Does not reach the hill stations, but can be found at lower elevations on the approaches.

Blue-throated Bee-eater

■ *Merops viridis* 23cm, plus tail spikes

DESCRIPTION Size similar to that of the Blue-tailed Bee-eater (see below). Brown cap, nape and mantle; black eye-stripe with red iris; bluish throat blending into light green chest and underparts; wing-coverts darker green, primaries and tail bluish-green. **DISTRIBUTION** From S China to SE Asia, Borneo and Java; resident but making substantial local movements. **HABITAT AND HABITS** Though commonly seen in open habitats such as beach scrub, former tin-mining areas, rice fields and open country, perched on utility lines and bare twigs, it also frequents forest edges and the canopy, particularly when lowland habitats are occupied by migrant Blue-tailed. Can be seen hawking insects from exposed perches to well above 1,000m, on approach roads to the hill stations.

Blue-tailed Bee-eater

■ *Merops philippinus* 24cm, plus tail spikes

DESCRIPTION Generally light green on upperparts, wings and underparts (grading into light blue at vent); white patch below bill; throat brownish-yellow; black eye-stripe with red iris; conspicuous bright blue tail with central streamer. **DISTRIBUTION** From India and S China, through SE Asia and New Guinea. Populations in Malaysia and Singapore are mainly passage migrants and winter visitors. **HABITAT AND HABITS** Usually seen in open areas such as beach scrub, open country, former tin-mining lands and rice fields. Individuals or groups often seen perched on utility lines, using the perch to sally in pursuit of winged insects. Also uses the same perch to disarm prey such as bees of their sting. Roosts in groups.

Dollarbird

■ *Eurystomus orientalis* 30cm

DESCRIPTION Dark brown head with prominent red bill and feet; dark bluish-green body with some bluish-purple streaks at neck. When in flight, white patches on wings visible. **DISTRIBUTION** Resident from India to SE Asia and Australia, augmented by migratory northern populations. **HABITAT AND HABITS** Commonly encountered singly in mangroves, beach scrub, plantations and open country, usually on prominent vantage points. Often uses these perches to hunt for prey by sallying to catch winged insects such as ants and termites.

Black-thighed Falconet ■ *Microhierax fringillarius* 16cm

DESCRIPTION One of the world's tiniest raptors. Mainly black above and white below; narrow white line behind eye curling round black cheek-patch; narrow white forehead, throat, breast and marks on tail. Belly and vent rufous, and in juveniles a rufous tinge to pale band from cheek to brow. **DISTRIBUTION** Lowlands of Malay Peninsula, Sumatra and Borneo (except Sabah), from sea level to about 900m. **HABITAT AND HABITS** Sociable, in loose family associations in the canopy of tall lowland rainforest, where individuals sit separately on bare exposed perches, visible to each other up to several hundred metres apart; they sometimes exchange perches, and share prey. Feeds on large insects (katydids, locusts, cicadas and butterflies), and occasionally small birds and mammals.

Peregrine Falcon ▪ *Falco peregrinus* 40–48cm

DESCRIPTION Large, dark falcon; resident race *F. p. ernesti* has a distinctive black hood. Upperparts and tail dark grey; throat and underparts cream with dark streaks and heavy barring. Juveniles of resident race rich rufous below, but distinguished from the **Oriental Hobby** *F. severus* (suspected but never confirmed from Fraser's Hill) by large size, and by barring rather than streaks below. Migrants paler, and hood is broken by pale cheeks separating dark moustache from rear part of head and neck. Narrow orbital ring and legs yellow; bill yellow at base and dark towards tip. **DISTRIBUTION** Global distribution. Resident in Peninsular Malaysia mainly near limestone cliffs; migrants more widespread throughout the area. **HABITAT AND HABITS** Usually solitary or in pairs, seen at limestone outcrops in forest and in open country, where residents are much outnumbered by migrants. Both residents and migrants recorded using city buildings in lieu of natural cliffs. Uses high vantage points to look out for prey – mainly smaller birds such as pigeons and waders, and sometimes bats – and hunts by diving and knocking them over in flight.

Blue-rumped Parrot ▪ *Psittinus cyanurus* 18cm

DESCRIPTION Quite a small, short-tailed parrot, green above and light green below. Male has blue rump, blue head, black upper back and red bill. Female's rump green; head and bill dull brown. Both sexes have dark red patch on shoulder and red underwing-coverts, often hidden but best seen in flight. **DISTRIBUTION** Malay Peninsula, Borneo and Sumatra, including various W Sumatran islands; resident. **HABITAT AND HABITS** Typically occurs in lowland dipterocarp forest, but wanders into logged forest, tree plantations and orchards, and upwards to about the elevation of The Gap below Fraser's Hill. Feeds in pairs or small parties in the canopy, taking fruits (including small amounts of oil palm).

Blue-crowned Hanging-parrot
■ *Loriculus galgulus* 14cm

DESCRIPTION Smallest parrot in the region, generally green in both sexes. In adult male, breast and rump red; yellow/orange patch on mantle; small blue crown. Female does not have blue crown and red breast-patch. **DISTRIBUTION** Malay Peninsula, Sumatra and Borneo. Resident in Malaysia and Singapore. **HABITAT AND HABITS** Typically confined to the canopy of trees in forests, forest edges and wooded gardens. Seldom descends low except to feed on small fruits and flower buds. Often vocal in flight. Interestingly, will hang upside down like a bat when roosting.

Long-tailed Broadbill ■ *Psarisomus dalhousiae* 26cm

DESCRIPTION Like a parakeet; brilliant grass-green bill and wings, paler turquoise on breast, bluer on primaries and long tail. Narrow white collar (perhaps better defined in female that in male) joins yellow throat, with yellow patch over ear; black sides and top of head, with little blue skull-cap. **DISTRIBUTION** Resident from C Himalayan foothills, through S China and Indochina, to Peninsular Malaysia, Sumatra and Borneo. Not found in Singapore. **HABITAT AND HABITS** Montane forest defines this bird's distribution to a maximum of 1,500m and down to about 850m, with scattered records as low as 250m in foothills. Occurs in small (family?) parties seeking insects on foliage and twigs of trees in middle and upper storeys, and occasionally in small trees along quiet forest roads. Flock members bob, flaunt tails and call to each other in descending series of trills.

Dusky Broadbill ■ *Corydon sumatranus* 25–30cm

DESCRIPTION Chunky, heavily built broadbill; dark chocolate-brown or blackish
with buff throat-patch, white flash on bases of primaries (best seen in flight), and
whitish tips to tail feathers. Tip of bill grey; rest of bill and skin around eye pale pink.
DISTRIBUTION Mainland SE Asia, to Malay Peninsula, Sumatra and Borneo; resident.
HABITAT AND HABITS Found in tall lowland forest, occasionally into montane
elevations, sitting in small family groups in the canopy, including on an exposed perch,
giving a variety of harsh and squeaky whistles. Rather uncommon but conspicuous once
it begins calling. Has been recorded at elevations below Fraser's Hill.

Silver-breasted Broadbill ■ *Serilophus lunatus* 16cm

DESCRIPTION Most elegant bird, with silvery-grey head and breast (crossed in female by silver-white line), shading to ashy-brown back and rich chestnut rump. Conspicuous black eyebrow, and black wings with flashes of blue and white. Bill silvery-blue and yellow.
DISTRIBUTION Resident from E Himalayas, through S China and Indo-Malayan region as far as Peninsular Malaysia and Sumatra (not Singapore or Borneo). **HABITAT AND HABITS** In Peninsular Malaysia only along Main Range, to about 1,200m and down to variable altitude, sometimes as low as 230m, in middle and lower storeys. Could be considered a hill-slope rather than strictly montane bird. Nest hung from small tree over hillside gully, the lining replenished with fresh green leaves throughout incubation as in other broadbills. Thought to feed on insects.

Banded Broadbill
■ *Eurylaimus javanicus* 22cm

DESCRIPTION Dusky red head, neck, breast and belly, with obscure, narrow grey band across breast; wings, back and tail black; many of back and wing feathers and rump with broad yellow streaks. Male darker about face than female, and has more strongly defined breast-band. Bill dull blue-grey in adults, yellowish-grey in juveniles, which have overall paler and browner plumage with fewer contrasting streaks. **DISTRIBUTION** SE Asia to Malay Peninsula, Sumatra, Borneo and Java; resident. **HABITAT AND HABITS** Found in the canopy of tall forest, usually in pairs, in lowlands and reaching lower montane elevations. Easily recognized song begins with an explosive trill, and settles to a slower rhythm of single notes that accelerate and fade away over several seconds.

Black-and-Yellow Broadbill ■ *Eurylaimus ochromalus* 15cm

DESCRIPTION Small broadbill with black head, white collar, conspicuous black breast-band (broken medially in female) and pale pink underparts; wings and tail largely black with multiple flashes of yellow on back, coverts, secondaries and rump. Comical yellow eye and blue bill. **DISTRIBUTION** Resident from central Thailand and Myanmar, through Peninsular Malaysia (not, or perhaps no longer, in Singapore), Sumatra, Belitung and Borneo. **HABITAT AND HABITS** Occurs in the canopy and middle storey of lowland forest, peat swamp and sometimes rubber plantations, though it may be hard to see. Song is like that of the Banded Broadbill (see above), but lacks the introductory trill, so begins slowly with a long series of notes, accelerating and rising until ending sharply. Bag-like dead-leaf nest is hung from a branch or twig, usually over a space beneath.

Rusty-naped Pitta ▪ *Pitta oatesi* 17cm

DESCRIPTION Bright rufous-cinnamon, darker on crown and breast, a little lighter on forehead and face; narrow black line behind eye almost to nape. Back and wing-coverts bright deep green, and tail bright blue-green. Bill grey, and long, strong legs dark pink. Juveniles darker than adults; grey-brown on head, dark brown above and below, lacking any cinnamon, green or blue but with scatter of white spots on underparts and wing-coverts. **DISTRIBUTION** Discontinuously through mainland SE Asia, from Himalayas to Malay Peninsula; resident. **HABITAT AND HABITS** Only confirmed in Malaysia in 1977, at Fraser's Hill, after decades of rumours about a resident pitta there. Has subsequently been recorded at Cameron Highlands and Genting Highlands. Occurs in understorey of lower montane forest, among the leaf litter or perched on logs or undergrowth, building an untidy ball nest of dead leaves. Call is a two-note whistle.

Blue-winged Pitta ▪ *Pitta moluccensis* 20cm

DESCRIPTION Brilliantly parti-coloured with black mask, buff underparts with red beneath tail, green upperparts and bright blue wings. In flight, wings are bold blue and black with white panels, like those of many pittas and some kingfishers. Two similar species are the big-billed **Mangrove Pitta** *P. megarhyncha* in Peninsular Malaysia and chestnut-crowned hillside **Fairy Pitta** *P. nympha* in Borneo. **DISTRIBUTION** Resident in China and Indochina south to N Peninsular Malaysia; migrant to rest of peninsula, Singapore, Sabah and Sarawak, occasionally reaching as far as Java. **HABITAT AND HABITS** Usually alone, in lowland forest or dense vegetation in plantations or even large gardens, where it hops on the ground, turning the leaf litter to seek insects and grubs. Migrates at night, and there are many records of birds stunned by hitting buildings when disorientated by lights. Call is a four-note *chew-chew; chew-chew*.

Blyth's Shrike-babbler ■ *Pteruthius aeralatus* 17cm

DESCRIPTION Entirely pearl-white undersides; crown and mask of male black with white eyebrow; grey back; black wings and tail; inner secondaries ochre and chestnut; tips of primaries white. Female has subdued grey head and back, and light olive-green wings and tail. **DISTRIBUTION** Resident from W Himalayan foothills, through S China, discontinuously to Peninsular Malaysia (not Singapore), Sumatra, Borneo and Java. **HABITAT AND HABITS** Confined to montane forest of Larut Range, Main Range and various outlying mountains, from 900m in tall lower montane forest to 2,000m in elfin upper montane vegetation, mainly in the canopy but also at forest edges. Territorial pairs call loudly, nesting in early February–June, on a branch at canopy or mid-level. Insectivore, known to take caterpillars and other invertebrates.

Black-eared Shrike-babbler ■ *Pteruthius melanotis* 12cm

DESCRIPTION All age and sex classes have black line before, around and behind eye, curling down around ear-coverts, emphasizing white eye-ring; green crown and back; wings blacker with two pale bars. Male has orange throat and yellow underparts; female and young have yellow ear-coverts and pearly breast. **DISTRIBUTION** Resident from C Himalayan foothills, through S China, discontinuously to Peninsular Malaysia (not Singapore). **HABITAT AND HABITS** Confined to montane forest of Main Range and various outlying mountains, at about 1,000–1,800m in tall forest, where it forages in the canopy and middle storey. Insectivore, known to take caterpillars and presumably other insects, searching foliage, lichen-covered branches and trunks for them. Call is a scolding trill.

White-bellied Erpornis ■ *Erpornis zantholeuca* 13cm

DESCRIPTION Pale grey face, breast and (nearly white) belly; crown with its short erectile crest, back, wings and tail light green, with yellow touch to fringes of primaries, and yellow beneath tail. Sexes alike. DISTRIBUTION Resident from W Himalayan foothills, through S China to Taiwan, and through SE Asia to Peninsular Malaysia (not Singapore), Sumatra and Borneo. HABITAT AND HABITS Formerly considered to be a yuhina, but now not even included among the babblers. Seen singly or in pairs in the crowns and middle storey of lowland evergreen rainforest from the extreme lowlands to around 900m, occasionally into lower montane forest to a maximum of 1,200m. Foliage-gleaning insectivore; persistent but still scarce participant in mixed foraging flocks.

Black-and-Crimson Oriole ■ *Oriolus cruentus* 22cm

DESCRIPTION Entirely black, except that male has brilliant crimson breast-patch and crimson primary wing-coverts; silvery-grey bill and grey feet. In female breast-patch may be faintly indicated by grey tone. DISTRIBUTION Resident in mountains of Peninsular Malaysia, Sumatra, Borneo and Java. HABITAT AND HABITS Occurs singly or in pairs in tall forest from 600m on hill slopes, to 1,500m in montane forest in the peninsula, to 2,300m in Borneo. Keeps largely to the canopy, sometimes in the middle storey and edges along quiet forested roadsides or tracks, taking foliage-eating caterpillars as well as other insects and some fruits. Cat-like mewing and harsh nasal notes have been described throughout its range; melodious call only mentioned from Borneo.

Dark-throated Oriole ■ *Oriolus xanthonotus* 18cm

DESCRIPTION Male has brilliant yellow back, rump and vent, with contrasting black head and upper breast, black wings and tail with yellow markings, and strongly streaked black-and-white abdomen. Female olive-green with strongly streaked black-and-white underparts, and yellow vent. Bill conspicuous pink in both sexes. DISTRIBUTION Malay Peninsula, Sumatra and its western islands, Borneo and Java. Resident in lowlands of Peninsular Malaysia, reaching to hill forest around The Gap below Fraser's Hill. HABITAT AND HABITS Found in middle and upper storeys of lowland forest and forest edges, occasionally into adjacent tree plantations, feeding on fruits (like figs), and insects and caterpillars, but more easily heard than seen. Fluty whistles reminiscent of the Black-naped Oriole's (see below), softer but varied. Recorded to about 1,200m, but more usual below 800m.

Black-naped Oriole ■ *Oriolus chinensis* 26cm

DESCRIPTION Male brilliant yellow over most of plumage; even the black wings and tail have yellow bars and flashes. Black band from bill through eye, joining at back of head. Bill rosy pink, feet grey. Female slightly duller, more olive above; juveniles olive-green, streaky below, with only faint indications of future adult pattern. DISTRIBUTION Naturally resident from Mongolia, discontinuously through E and SE Asia, to Lesser Sunda Islands. Migrant to much of SE Asia, including Peninsular Malaysia, Singapore and rarely Borneo, plus natural and human-assisted spread of residents through Singapore and Peninsular Malaysia since 1925. HABITAT AND HABITS Gardens, parkland, orchards and secondary woodland in lowlands are preferred habitats, where it forages for all sorts of fruits and insects; also mangroves. There is much interaction between individuals, with loud, fluting calls, *ku-eyouou*, instantly recognizable but tremendously variable, and chasing, following and displacement from food sources.

Bar-winged Flycatcher-shrike
■ *Hemipus picatus* 15cm

DESCRIPTION Black cap and mask, bordered with white below; smoky-grey breast and belly; black wings and tail, with long, clear white wing-bar from carpals across coverts to tips of secondaries. Female browner above and paler below than male, and in juveniles wing-bar is buff. **DISTRIBUTION** S and SE Asia, to Malay Peninsula, Sumatra and Borneo; resident. **HABITAT AND HABITS** Occurs in hill dipterocarp and lower montane forests from 500m upwards, sometimes in rubber and other plantations, often moving through middle storey with other birds in mixed foraging flocks, or in pairs. Has been recorded at all three hill stations along the Main Range.

Black-winged Flycatcher-shrike ■ *Hemipus hirundinaceus* 15cm

DESCRIPTION Male has black face and crown, neck, back, wings and tail; pure white rump; pearly-grey to white underparts from chin to vent. Female like male but duller and browner. **DISTRIBUTION** From about 7° N southwards through Malay Peninsula, Sumatra, Borneo and intervening islands, Java and Bali. Resident in Peninsular Malaysia, Sabah and Sarawak; never reliably recorded from Singapore. **HABITAT AND HABITS** Inhabits lowland forest, swamp forest and landward side of mangroves from sea level to about 300m, rarely to 800m; in upper storey, or lower at the forest edge. Usually occurs as a pair or alone, flycatching and gleaning foliage for insects. Call is a short, fairly harsh trill.

Large Woodshrike
■ *Tephrornis virgatus* 22cm

DESCRIPTION Grey and white, with striking black mask through eye. Corwn, back and wings grey, tail and wing-tips black; throat, belly and vent white, washed with pale grey across breast; rump white. Forehead distinctly pale in male, less so in female. **DISTRIBUTION** S, SE and E Asia, to Malay Peninsula, Sumatra, Borneo, Java and Bali; resident. **HABITAT AND HABITS** Found in lowland and hill forests and forest edges, up to lower montane elevations. Can occur in pairs or in small parties, seeking insects among foliage and twigs, but is not common. Calls include a series of quick, piping notes, all on the same pitch or of shifting pitch and volume.

Maroon-breasted Philentoma

■ *Philentoma velata* 20cm

DESCRIPTION Stocky fly-catching passerine, the male overall deep matt blue, with black face and throat merging into deep maroon breast-patch. Female similar but duller blue, with dark sides of face and throat; rump, abdomen and undertail-coverts bluish-grey. Both sexes have reddish eyes. **DISTRIBUTION** Malay Peninsula, Sumatra, Borneo and Java; resident. **HABITAT AND HABITS** Occurs in lower and middle storeys of lowland and hill forests; occasionally recorded to 1,700m, and seen at lower elevations on approaches to the hill stations (such as The Gap and Ginting Simpah) and potentially occurring higher. Call a single musical whistle, and a harsh *churr*; also a long series of spaced, descending, bell-like notes; these calls are often intermixed.

Common Iora ■ *Aegithina tiphia* 13cm

DESCRIPTION Green above with black tail and (in male) black on crown; yellow below, fading to white on undertail-coverts that curl sideways and up over rump to make rump seem white; wings black with two white bars and pale fringes. **DISTRIBUTION** W Himalayas to India, Sri Lanka and S China, to Peninsular Malaysia, Singapore, Sumatra and offliers, Borneo, Java, Bali and the Philippines; resident. **HABITAT AND HABITS** In display flight from tree to tree male displays his false white rump, while singing: the species has a huge range of calls and song types. Takes insects from foliage in mangroves and back-mangroves, plantations, trees in parks and roadsides, and entering the edges of lowland evergreen forest. Often forages high in the canopy, for example in tall *Albizia* trees, but also comes down to the understorey. Breeds in January–June.

Malaysian Cuckoo-shrike ■ *Coracina larutensis* 28cm

DESCRIPTION Previously called *C. novaehollandiae/javensis*. Subtly shaded ash-grey all over, darkest on face and around base of bill, palest on belly and beneath tail; robust black bill and legs. **DISTRIBUTION** Resident from W Himalayas, through S China to Taiwan, and SE Asia to Peninsular Malaysia (only), Java and Bali. Other cuckoo-shrike species occur in lowland forest of Peninsular Malaysia, and lowland and montane forests of Sabah and Sarawak. **HABITAT AND HABITS** Occurs singly or in pairs in the canopy of montane forest, at 1,000–2,050m, foraging for small, round fruits and arthropods among foliage, and taking some insects in flight. Nest is a deep cup of twigs and lichen in a horizontal fork of a branch. Has an amusing habit of alternately lifting each folded wing.

Lesser Cuckoo-shrike
■ *Lalage fimbriata* 20cm

DESCRIPTION Smart and slim. Male dark grey all over, appearing black in poor light, with slightly paler rump and undertail-coverts, and white tips visible only on underside of tail. Female pale ash-grey, nearly white below and on face, the entire underparts finely but distinctly barred with black. Lores to eye black. **DISTRIBUTION** Malay Peninsula to Borneo, Sumatra, Java and Bali; resident. **HABITAT AND HABITS** Seen in forest to 1,000m, occasionally higher, singly or in pairs or small (family?) parties, in upper and middle storeys. Known to participate in mixed foraging flocks, but not a common bird.

Fiery Minivet ■ *Pericrocotus igneus* 16cm

DESCRIPTION Confusingly like other minivets. Male distinguished from the Grey-chinned Minivet (see below) by its blacker chin and throat, and from the Scarlet Minivet (see p. 86) by a smaller wing-patch, tinged orange. Female more easily distinguished, with yellow throat and face like Scarlet's, but no separate yellow patch on tertiaries; orange-red (not yellow) rump; wing-patch also tinged orange. **DISTRIBUTION** Malay Peninsula, Sumatra and offlying islands, Borneo and Palawan; resident. **HABITAT AND HABITS** Found in hilly forest in lowlands, extending into lower montane forest and forest edges, usually high in trees, moving through and above the canopy. Occurs in small parties or sometimes in pairs, giving very high-pitched, twittering calls. Recorded from Fraser's Hill but apparently not yet the other hill stations.

Grey-chinned Minivet ■ *Pericrocotus solaris* 18cm

DESCRIPTION Adult male black and red; chin only slightly greyer than head; single long red wing-bar; the male Scarlet Minivet (see p. 86) has separate red wing-spot on tertiaries, and the Fiery Minivet (see above) is slightly smaller with a different flight call (an upwards slurred *swee-eet*). Female of similar pattern, but dark grey and yellow, with dark grey forehead and white chin. **DISTRIBUTION** From C Himalayan foothills, through S China to Taiwan, and in highlands south to Peninsular Malaysia (not Singapore), Sumatra and Borneo; resident. **HABITAT AND HABITS** Seen in the crowns of tall trees in lower and upper montane forests, at 975–2,075m, into stunted elfin forest. Searches for insects in foliage while perched, and hovers at shoot-tips. Occurs in pairs, and outside February–April breeding season, in flocks of up to 30. Flight call a repeated twittering, *sri-sisi*.

Scarlet Minivet ■ *Pericrocotus flammeus* 19cm

DESCRIPTION Male black and red, very like the Grey-chinned Minivet (see p. 85), but with a second, small, rounded patch of red on secondaries. Female grey and yellow, paler

than female Grey-chinned, with second (yellow) wing-patch and yellowish forehead. **DISTRIBUTION** Resident from W Himalayas and Indian subcontinent, through S China and SE Asia, to Peninsular Malaysia, Singapore, Sumatra, Belitung, Borneo and the Philippines, to Java, Bali and Lombok. **HABITAT AND HABITS** Like other minivets, prefers the crowns of tall trees, in this case in lowland evergreen rainforest from the extreme lowlands to about 1,000m (just into lower montane forest, overlapping with Grey-chinned), and in peat-swamp forest. Takes all sorts of small invertebrates. Pairs after breeding (January–June) group into flocks.

Ashy Minivet

■ *Pericrocotus divaricatus* 19cm

DESCRIPTION Small black-and-white bird, longer and slimmer than the **Pied Triller** *Lalage nigra*, with short, narrow white brow and long, narrow white wing-bar (not a broad panel). Sexes alike. **DISTRIBUTION** Breeds from Siberia, through N China to Korea and Japan; winters south to India, SE Asia, including Peninsular Malaysia, Singapore, Sabah and Sarawak, to the Philippines. **HABITAT AND HABITS** Non-breeding birds characteristic of coastal forest, but also occur in the canopy of lowland and peat-swamp forest, occasionally up into lower montane forest. Flocks of 20 or more trickle from tree to tree, follow-my-leader fashion, uttering soft, tinkling notes, and foraging for insects before moving on.

White-throated Fantail ■ *Rhipidura albicollis* 19cm

DESCRIPTION Blackish above and below, except for white throat-triangle, white brow and white tips to tail feathers. Juveniles duller and browner than adults, with brow and throat mark less well defined. **DISTRIBUTION** Resident from W Himalayas, to S China and SE Asia, to Peninsular Malaysia (not in Singapore), Sumatra and Borneo. **HABITAT AND HABITS** Confined to lower montane forest, usually about 850m upwards into upper montane forest at 2,070m maximum. In middle and lower storeys, seeks insects and is one of the most common birds, with a repeated, tuneful song of 7–8 notes. Common participant in mixed foraging flocks. Nest is a cup slung in the fork of a small lateral branch in the middle storey, hardly big enough to contain two growing young.

Crow-billed Drongo ■ *Dicrurus annectens* 28cm

DESCRIPTION Entirely black, glossy plumage, with spreading forked 'fish-tail', the points of outer rectrices curved out and slightly upwards. Juveniles have a little pale spotting on breast and belly. Bill heavy and robust with basal bristles; eyes and feet dark. The similar **Black Drongo** *D. macrocercus* at low elevations (not highlands) has more deeply forked tail and prefers more open habitats. **DISTRIBUTION** From Himalayas to Borneo and Java; here a passage migrant and winter visitor. Occasional at lower elevations of hills and lower montane forest. **HABITAT AND HABITS** Found in hill forest to about 1,000m on migration, within or at edges of dense vegetation. Utters varied rasping and twanging call notes.

Bronzed Drongo ▪ *Dicrurus aeneus* 24cm

DESCRIPTION Like the Crow-billed Drongo (see p. 87) but smaller, with slightly more delicate bill, and less upturned outer tips of tail. Very black face, somewhat set off against glossy spangled breast and glossy crown and back. **DISTRIBUTION** S, SE and E Asia, through Malay Peninsula, to Sumatra and Borneo; resident. **HABITAT AND HABITS** Occurs singly, in pairs or less often in small parties, in middle storey of tall forest in lowlands, reaching into lower montane forest, so that it has been recorded on the approaches to all three hill stations. Flies out from an open perch to snap up insects in flight or from foliage. Bathes by diving from perch into a forest pool.

Lesser Racket-tailed Drongo
▪ *Dicrurus remifer* 25–65cm

DESCRIPTION A little smaller than other drongos, and if tail rackets are present, then easily distinguished – wires are very long (to 40cm), and rackets are elongated and narrow. If tail rackets are absent, look for square (not forked) tip of tail, bill smaller than in Greater Racket-tailed Drongo (see opposite) and heavy bristles at base of bill. **DISTRIBUTION** India to Australia and extreme W Pacific. Resident in mountains of Peninsular Malaysia, including all the Main Range hill stations and various isolated peaks. **HABITAT AND HABITS** Occurs in middle and upper storeys of upper hill dipterocarp, lower montane and upper montane forests, from about 900m upwards. Found singly or in pairs, which often participate in mixed foraging flocks, hawking insects from a lookout perch.

Greater Racket-tailed Drongo

■ *Dicrurus paradiseus* 32–57cm

DESCRIPTION Noisy, conspicuous, glossy black bird with red eye; two outer tail feathers project as wires, with one rounded and twisted racket on each side. One or both rackets may be missing due to moult or damage. **DISTRIBUTION** Resident from Indian subcontinent, eastwards to Hainan, through Peninsular Malaysia and Singapore, to Sumatra, Borneo, Java and Bali. **HABITAT AND HABITS** Found in the canopy and middle storey of lowland evergreen rainforest from extreme lowlands to about 850m (for instance at The Gap and Ginting Simpah), and in mangroves, tree plantations (rubber and oil palm), parkland with abundant trees and secondary woodland. Typically seen in pairs and gives a wide range of calls, including good imitations of many other birds. Flies out from a high perch to catch passing insects.

Black-naped Monarch ■ *Hypothymis azurea* 16cm

DESCRIPTION Bright blue forequarters shading down to ashy-brown wings and tail, and whitish belly. Male has black throat-bar, crown-spot and dab over bill; female has greyer breast and black dab over bill. **DISTRIBUTION** Resident from India, through S China and SE Asia, to Peninsular Malaysia (and formerly Singapore), and to Borneo, the Philippines and Lesser Sunda Islands.

HABITAT AND HABITS Occurs in lower and middle storeys of lowland evergreen rainforest from extreme lowlands to about 915m in the peninsula, or to 1,100–1,200m in Sabah and Sarawak. Usually alone, or in pairs or mixed foraging flocks. One of the most common birds glimpsed during journeys along forested rivers, engaging in aerial flycatching within the forest and occasionally bathing by diving into the water.

Japanese Paradise Flycatcher ■ *Terpsiphone atrocaudata* 20–35cm

DESCRIPTION Male largely black, with purple-glossed back and wings, and white belly. Tail very long, black; prominent bare blue eye-ring. Female dark grey on head, neck and upper breast; blacker on crown; white lower breast to vent; rufous-brown back, wings and tail (less foxy-rufous than Blyth's Paradise-flycatcher, see opposite). **DISTRIBUTION** E and NE Asia, wintering south to the Philippines, Malay Peninsula, Sumatra and W Java, and once in Borneo; migrant in region. **HABITAT AND HABITS** Occurs in middle storey and crowns of tall trees, not deep in forest but near forest edges or in plantations and secondary woodland. Rather scarce as a migrant and possibly declining.

Blyth's Paradise Flycatcher
■ *Terpsiphone affinis* 22–40cm

DESCRIPTION Female has black cowl shading down to grey neck and breast, to whitish belly; rufous-chestnut wings and tail. Male either similar with an extremely long tail (nearly triple body length); or else body, wings and tail are pure white with fine black edgings to some feathers. Significance of male colour types unclear, but may not be age related. **DISTRIBUTION** Resident through C Asia to Korea, and south to Peninsular Malaysia, Singapore, Sumatra, Borneo, Java and Lesser Sunda Islands; non-breeding migrants also reach much of SE Asia. **HABITAT AND HABITS** White-phase male is truly spectacular; not a rare bird, resident in middle and upper storeys of tall lowland forest. Migrants also occur in tall secondary woodland. They are insectivores, usually solitary, taking fairly big insects, and live from extreme lowlands to about 880m in the peninsula; recorded higher elsewhere.

Tiger Shrike ■ *Lanius tigrinus* 18cm

DESCRIPTION Back, wings and tail rich brown; back and lesser wing-coverts always finely barred black. Strong contrast between brown back and grey cap; black mask and relatively thick bill. Female may show some barring on flanks. **DISTRIBUTION** Resident in far eastern Russia, Japan and Korea, through central China; non-breeding migrant to S China and SE Asia as far as Java and Bali. **HABITAT AND HABITS** Found in forest edges, bamboo groves, dense roadside vegetation and abandoned cultivation, extending into heavily logged forest. Noted singly throughout Peninsular Malaysia, Singapore, Sabah and Sarawak to about 850m, but most Borneo records are only from the north. Beetles and grasshoppers are the chief prey.

Brown Shrike ■ *Lanius cristatus* 19cm

DESCRIPTION Several subspecies differ in tone, but always have plain back, never finely barred. Black mask, pale supercilium and either brown or grey crown; back and tail brown; undersides off white; bill relatively small. Sexes alike. **DISTRIBUTION** Resident through vast areas of temperate E Asia, from 70° E to Sakhalin and south through China; migrates to China, India and SE Asia as far as Sumatra, Borneo, the Philippines, Java and Lesser Sunda Islands. **HABITAT AND HABITS** In our non-breeding range, arriving birds set up territories in cultivated areas, gardens, and open ground with bushes, scattered trees and grassland, advertising with chattering calls around September arrival and March departure. Occurs singly, on fences, trees and bush tops, descending to catch invertebrates on the ground, mostly beetles and grasshoppers but occasionally lizards and small birds.

Long-tailed Shrike ■ *Lanius schach* 26cm

DESCRIPTION Black mask extending over forehead; underparts white with peach-buff flanks; crown and back grey, merging to buff on scapulars. Long tail and blackish wings

show strong contrast with body, with white wing-spot best visible in flight. **DISTRIBUTION** Resident from Kyrgyzstan, through C Asia and Indian subcontinent, to all but N China, patchily through SE Asia to Java, Bali, Lesser Sunda Islands and New Guinea. Northern populations migrate, a few as far as Borneo. **HABITAT AND HABITS** Spread of cultivation suggests possible arrival of this bird in Peninsular Malaysia in the second half of the 19th century. Still only found west of Main Range but commonly in Singapore; in Sabah and Sarawak it is just a scarce migrant. Occurs in open rice fields and grassland with shrubs, taking mainly insects.

Jay Shrike
■ *Platylophus galericulatus* 32cm

DESCRIPTION Blackish all over, and proportionately rather large head bearing a fine vertical or forwards-tilting crest; white marks around eye and white patch on sides of neck. **DISTRIBUTION** Resident from about 13° N in peninsular Thailand, through Malaysia (but not Singapore), to Sumatra, Borneo and Java. **HABITAT AND HABITS** Not easy to see, but it can be curious, raising a shrike-like, rattling chatter when it sees people. Keeps to middle and lower storeys of lowland evergreen rainforest; rarely in montane forest to 1,200m in Peninsular Malaysia, and a record at 1,525m in Sarawak. Usually solitary or in pairs, seeking invertebrates: beetles, grasshoppers, wasps, cicadas and others. Nest has only been described recently, from a single observation in Java.

Common Green Magpie ■ *Cissa chinensis* 38cm

DESCRIPTION Brilliant lime-green plumage with bright red bill and feet; black mask through eye to nape; chestnut wings tipped black and white on secondaries; tapered tail tipped black and white. **DISTRIBUTION** Resident, from Himalayas to Borneo. In Peninsular Malaysia found along Main Range, including at all three hill stations, and various outlying mountains. **HABITAT AND HABITS** Occurs in middle storey of montane forest, occasionally up into high canopy and down almost to ground level, from about 900m to 1,800m. Often hard to see despite bright colouring. Occasionally vociferous, with a series of harsh chatters followed by a whistle, or uttering the whistle and chatters separately.

Sunda Crow ■ *Corvus enca* 45cm

DESCRIPTION Slimly built, all-black crow with square-ended tail and (compared with other crows locally) slender bill only slightly arched. In flight, shows square tail (rounded when spread) and blunt wings; often gives brief display flights with shivering wings and twanging call. **DISTRIBUTION** Sunda subregion, from S Thailand to Java and Bali. Similar-looking crows from the Philippines, Sulawesi and Seram are now split off into other species. **HABITAT AND HABITS** True forest crow, occurring in small parties (2–4 birds) in the canopy. Usually found below 900m, and may be heard or perhaps seen near access roads to the hill stations. Assumed to feed on a range of fruits, invertebrates and possibly small vertebrates; rarely ventures into adjacent tall tree plantations.

Southern Jungle Crow ■ *Corvus macrorhynchos* 50cm

DESCRIPTION Big (raven-sized), glossy black crow with heavy, arched bill bearing bristles at base; tail long and wedge shaped. **DISTRIBUTION** Mainland SE Asia and Peninsular Malaysia, discontinuously to Sumatra, Java, Lesser Sundas and the Philippines. Now split

off from similar-looking crows through much of Asia (Iran to India and China) that have differing habits (voice, flocking) and differ genetically. **HABITAT AND HABITS** Found in forest edges and disturbed environments with many trees (rubber, oil palm, secondary tree growth), mostly in lowlands but occasionally to 1,800m at hill stations. More likely in agricultural areas of Cameron Highlands than at other hill stations. Call a deep *kronk*, lower pitched than calls of other crows. Never in large flocks; often seen singly or in small parties.

House Crow ■ *Corvus splendens* 42cm

DESCRIPTION Glossy black plumage, progressively with age developing greyish nape, face behind eye and breast. Distinguished from the Southern Jungle Crow (see opposite) by size and smaller bill, and from that and the **Sunda Crow** *C. enca* by habits, voice and grey plumage features. **DISTRIBUTION** Naturally occurring from Iran to China, now spreading widely to Indonesia, Australasia and parts of Europe through deliberate and accidental introductions acting as nuclei for further spread. Introduced to Peninsular Malaysia about 1903. **HABITAT AND HABITS** Occurs in big urban roosts in many west-coast towns, dispersing during the day to forage in open, man-made environments, villages, plantations, farmland and rubbish dumps. Recorded from various parts of Cameron Highlands to high elevations, but not yet at Fraser's Hill.

Rail Babbler ■ *Eupetes macrocerus* 28cm

DESCRIPTION Cinnamon-brown, ground-living bird with long, slender tail; crown, throat and breast brighter brown; forehead yellowish; broad white stripe above eye and black stripe through eye; bright blue skin (visible or hidden) on sides of neck. Sexes alike. Juveniles duller than adults, with pale throat. **DISTRIBUTION** Malay Peninsula, Sumatra and Borneo; resident. **HABITAT AND HABITS** Present in tall forest from extreme lowlands, through hill forest into lower montane elevations. Moves elusively through understorey vegetation, and best identified by song. Gives single, steady pure whistles, fading in and fading away, very like but slightly higher pitched than the **Garnet Pitta's** *Pitta granatina*, at regular intervals of about 10 seconds. Noted below Fraser's Hill.

Grey-headed Canary-flycatcher
■ *Culicicapa ceylonensis* 12cm

DESCRIPTION Grey head, throat and upper breast; remainder of underparts rather bright greeny-yellow; back and wings olive-green. Sexes alike. **DISTRIBUTION** Resident from Himalayas, through S and C China, south to Peninsular Malaysia (not Singapore), Sumatra, Borneo, Java and Lesser Sunda Islands to Flores. **HABITAT AND HABITS** Call of four notes in two couplets is usually followed by a fifth note. Probably territorial pairs found in middle storey from the plains in lowland evergreen rainforest to at least 1,700m in tall upper montane forest. Usually not shy, flycatching from regular perches. In Borneo is a brood host of the parasitic **Hodgson's Hawk-cuckoo** *Hierococcyx nisicolor*.

Sultan Tit ■ *Melanochlora sultanea* 18cm

DESCRIPTION Heavily built and strong-billed tit. Male has black head, upper breast, wings and tail; striking erect, shaggy yellow crest; yellow lower breast, belly and undertail-

coverts. Female similar, but areas that are black in male (face, wings, upper breast) are brownish-black to olive-brown. **DISTRIBUTION** From Himalayas to Peninsular Malaysia; resident. **HABITAT AND HABITS** Known from a range of forest types, including freshwater swamp forest, and lowland and hill forests, to about 1,200m in lower montane forest; best glimpsed from roadsides or tracks giving views into upper storey. Call an attractive repeated, modulated whistle.

Asian House Martin
■ *Delichon dasypus* 13cm

DESCRIPTION In flight, wings entirely dark above and below; black crown, face and upperparts, glossed blue, with pure white rump, and pure white underparts from chin to vent. Tail quite short but clearly forked. **DISTRIBUTION** From Himalayas to N and E Asia, wintering south to S and SE Asia, Malay Peninsula, Sumatra, Borneo and Java; migrant in region. **HABITAT AND HABITS** Noted occasionally at montane elevations, from all three of the hill stations, most often in flight when hawking for insects with other swallows or with swiftlets. Occasionally seen perched on wires, aerials or buildings.

Rufous-bellied Swallow ■ *Cecropis badia* 18–20cm

DESCRIPTION Notably big swallow found in Peninsular Malaysia. Deep, evenly brick-red over face, entire underparts and broad, square rump; crown, nape, back, wings and tail blackish with rich blue gloss. Juveniles slightly duller than adults. **DISTRIBUTION** Endemic to Malay Peninsula; also potentially in Sumatra. Brick-red form may intergrade with the Daurian Swallow (see p. 98), with a pale streaky breast, which occurs as a scarce migrant to region and is resident in Java and Lesser Sunda Islands. **HABITAT AND HABITS** Cliff nester, foraging to many kilometres beyond these breeding sites, over numerous types of forest and cultivated area. At Fraser's Hill, individuals probably nesting at limestone outcrops in lowlands to the east, near Raub, come up to montane altitudes daily to forage, interspersed with the more common Barn Swallows (see p. 99). Size, colour and strongly triangular wings readily distinguish them.

Daurian Swallow ■ *Cecropis daurica* 16–20cm

DESCRIPTION Dark blue crown, wings and deeply forked tail; sides of face and underparts mealy-white, narrowly streaked blackish. Distinct square patch on rump (and, depending on race, patch on nape) orange-rufous in adults, buff in juveniles. **DISTRIBUTION** Resident from C Asia to Himalayas, Japan and Korea; Asian birds migrate to Peninsular Malaysia, Borneo and Sumatra, and perhaps further. **HABITAT AND HABITS** Occurs from sea-level back-mangroves to 1,250m over forested mountains, but mostly in open coastal plains, cultivated areas, grassland and scrub. Occasional birds can be picked out from wintering Barn Swallows (see opposite) by their more deliberate flight and obvious rump colour. Has become increasingly common over the past 30–40 years.

Pacific Swallow
■ *Hirundo tahitica* 14cm

DESCRIPTION Small swallow with reddish forehead, throat and upper breast, transitting directly to sullied greyish-white underparts; crown, back, wings and tail (with whitish spots) dark blue-black. Juveniles duller than adults, and browner, with less rufous on forehead and throat. On the wing it is smaller, dirtier looking and with a short, forked tail compared with the Barn Swallow (see opposite) **DISTRIBUTION** Resident from India, S China and Taiwan, throughout SE Asia, to New Guinea and W Pacific. **HABITAT AND HABITS** Abundant throughout region at all times of year. Often perches on wires and twigs, though not in large flocks, and spends most time on the wing, flying energetically over coasts and islands, open country, mangroves and forest edges. Mud nests built under bridges, or sometimes roof overhangs and other buildings, mostly in February–June.

Barn Swallow ■ *Hirundo rustica* 15–20cm

DESCRIPTION Larger swallow with black band between reddish upper breast and clean white, buff or pinkish underparts; upperparts and tail (with whitish spots) dark blue-black; tail deeply forked, with long streamers often missing during moult. **DISTRIBUTION** Resident almost throughout northern hemisphere, in Asia southwards to N Thailand and Vietnam; non-breeding migrant to all southern continents and throughout region. **HABITAT AND HABITS** A few individuals are present in almost every month, but predominantly seen in August–April, sometimes gathering in huge flocks, especially when roosting on overhead wires in well-lit, busy small towns. Numbers have declined over the decades, but still considered common. Not hard to identify by size, clean appearance and tail shape. Feeding birds may displace smaller Pacific Swallows (see opposite).

Ochraceous Bulbul ■ *Alophoixus ochraceus* 20cm

DESCRIPTION One of the larger bulbuls, with strong bill; grey-brown above and below, slightly greyer on sides of head; throat white and often puffed out; short, erectile crest rufous or ochre-brown. Sexes alike. **DISTRIBUTION** Resident in S Indochina, and from about 14° N in peninsular Thailand, Peninsular Malaysia, Sumatra and Borneo. **HABITAT AND HABITS** In continental Asia a lowland bird, but in Peninsular Malaysia, Sabah and Sarawak confined to slopes and mountains, from about 700m upwards. Utters a range of hoarse and sweet notes delivered in a rather random series, and occurs in pairs, often in association with mixed foraging flocks in middle storey of montane forest. Breeding occurs in about February–July.

Buff-vented Bulbul ■ *Iole charlottae* 20cm

DESCRIPTION Rather plain brown above; sides of face greyer, merging into pale throat, and dirty-buff breast and belly; pale iris and hint of eye-stripe and crown-stripes. Iris brown in juveniles. Locally the **Cream-vented Bulbul** *Pycnonotus simplex* also has pale eye, but plain crown without streaking or vague eye-stripe, and appears small headed. **DISTRIBUTION** Malay Peninsula, Sumatra, Borneo and intervening islands; resident. **HABITAT AND HABITS** Found within lowland forest, usually in middle storey, but also reaches to upper and lower storeys. Occurs to about the elevation of The Gap; not yet recorded at the other hill stations.

Cinereous Bulbul ■ *Hemixos cinereus* 21cm

DESCRIPTION Largely grey, with puffy white throat often highly visible, and contrasting darker moustache that merges upwards into grey sides of face; crown feathers erectile. Sexes alike. **DISTRIBUTION** Resident discontinuously to peninsular Thailand, Malaysia, Singapore, Sumatra and Borneo. Birds from C Himalayan foothills through S China and Indohina are now separated as the **Ashy Bulbul** *H. flavala*. **HABITAT AND HABITS**

Small flocks often seen, churring to each other as they puff out their throat feathers. Lives in forest on slopes from around 400m, through lower and upper montane forests to around 2,000m, occasionally making long-distance dispersal movements into lowlands, even as far as Singapore. Feeds on flying insects, and fruits taken while perched or snatched in flight. Nesting may occur in February–July.

Mountain Bulbul
■ *Hypsipetes mcclellandii* 22cm

DESCRIPTION Sturdy bulbul, common though not very well studied, with olive-green back, wings and tail, pale grey breast and bushy head, the crown feathers brown with pale central streaks. Sexes alike. **DISTRIBUTION** Resident from C Himalayas, through S China to Hainan, and parts of Indochina and Thailand to C Peninsular Malaysia. **HABITAT AND HABITS** In Peninsular Malaysia confined to montane forest of Main Range, Larut, Mt Tahan and a few outliers. Fairly common bulbul at about 100–2,100m, in the canopy of the forest and forest edges, often among mixed foraging flocks. Various small fruits comprise bulk of its food, with some insects. Occurs in pairs or small groups, nesting around March–May.

Streaked Bulbul ■ *Ixos malaccensis* 23cm

DESCRIPTION Gives appearance of a cool grey bird, becoming almost white on belly and undertail-coverts; sides of head, throat and upper breast with pale streaks on centre of each feather. Sexes alike. **DISTRIBUTION** Resident from about 12° 30' N in Myanmar, Peninsular Malaysia (and one doubtful record from Singapore), Sumatra, Lingga, Bangka and Borneo. **HABITAT AND HABITS** Occurs in the forest canopy of lowland evergreen rainforest, up slopes and just reaching into montane forest at around 1,100m. Figs of various species are commonly eaten; also flying insects such as termite swarms. Because of its preference for canopy-level perches it is often overlooked, and nesting is virtually unknown.

Black-crested Bulbul ■ *Pycnonotus flaviventris* 19cm

DESCRIPTION Dull olive-green above; olive-yellow below; entire head and throat black; iris cream, and black vertical crest. Endemic **Bornean Crested Bulbul** *P. montis* is almost the same, but with yellow throat. **DISTRIBUTION** Resident from C Himalayan foothills and Indian subcontinent, through SE Asia including Peninsular Malaysia (not Singapore except for a few escapees) and Sumatra. **HABITAT AND HABITS** Though a lowland bird in northern part of its range, largely confined to foothills and slopes in Peninsular Malaysia, in lowland evergreen forest mostly at 200–1,970m, well into upper montane forest. Seen singly or in pairs, flying out to snap at passing insects, and taking varied small fruits, including figs. Breeds in around January–July. Nests in dense forest-edge creepers and climbers such as bracken.

Scaly-breasted Bulbul
■ *Pycnonotus squamatus* 15cm

DESCRIPTION Small bulbul with scaly, dusky breast, black-and-white head and olive-yellow wings; undertail-coverts yellow. Sexes alike. **DISTRIBUTION** Resident in peninsular Thailand and Malaysia from about 8° N; not in Singapore, but in Sumatra, Borneo (including Sabah and Sarawak) and W Java. **HABITAT AND HABITS** Lowland evergreen rainforests on hill slopes to about 890m form the typical habitat of this delicate-looking bulbul, which feeds on small forest fruits, soft figs and possibly insects. It moves in the tree crowns, rarely low down. Reputed to have a cheerful whistling song, a repeated pretty trill, but the bird is poorly known and breeding has never been described.

Stripe-throated Bulbul
■ *Pycnonotus finlaysoni* 19cm

DESCRIPTION At first glance rather an ordinary brown bulbul, but bright yellow undertail-coverts, and in particular heavy yellow flecking on forehead and crown, ear-coverts, throat and upper breast, are very attractive. Sexes alike. DISTRIBUTION Resident from Yunnan in S China, through Myanmar, Thailand and Indochina, to Peninsular Malaysia; not in Singapore, Sabah or Sarawak. HABITAT AND HABITS In the north of range comes down into lowlands, but in Peninsular Malaysia largely confined to hill and montane forests; hence, from sea level upwards in Thailand, but mostly at 400–1,750m towards centre and south of peninsula, feeding on fruits and insects. Nests in small bushes, February–August.

Yellow-vented Bulbul
■ *Pycnonotus goiavier* 20cm

DESCRIPTION Pale below (breast whiter than in the **Flavescent Bulbul** P. *flavescens*) and brown above, with yellow undertail-coverts; black line from bill to eye, and narrow blackish strip along crown including short, erectile crest. Sexes alike. DISTRIBUTION Resident from about 12° 30' N in Myanmar, Indochina, peninsular Thailand, and Malaysia, Singapore, Sumatra, Java, Bali, Borneo and the Philippines. HABITAT AND HABITS One of the most common garden birds throughout the region, feeding on fruits of plants around cultivation – figs, *Lantana*, *Melastoma*, over-ripe papayas and many others – as well as occurring in cultivation and invading forest edges along roads into the highlands. Cheerful simple song, and often seen to lift both wings when landing on overhead wires.

Olive-winged Bulbul
■ *Pycnonotus plumosus* 20cm

DESCRIPTION Slightly larger than the Yellow-vented Bulbul (see p. 103), and rather plain brown above and below; brown wings but with a more olive-yellow obscure panel on folded wing; ear-coverts faintly streaked. Sexes alike. **DISTRIBUTION** Resident from about 12° 30' N in Myanmar, peninsular Thailand and Malaysia, Singapore including many offshore islands, Sumatra, Borneo, Java and Palawan. **HABITAT AND HABITS** Found throughout lowlands to about 500m, in forest edges and along logging tracks, but not in undisturbed forest; in scrub, coastal vegetation and tree plantations. Seen singly or in pairs, or with young. Feeds on small fruits, including figs, in dense, tangled vegetation. Never in big flocks. Nesting occurs in January–June.

Red-eyed Bulbul
■ *Pycnonotus brunneus* 19cm

DESCRIPTION Brown above and below, warmer on breast, paler on throat and undertail-coverts; iris red. Sexes alike. **DISTRIBUTION** Resident from around 12° 30' N in Myanmar, peninsular Thailand and Malaysia, scarce in Singapore, to Sumatra and offshore islands, and Borneo. **HABITAT AND HABITS** One of many common bulbul species that come together to feed on abundant fruits of figs in the middle storey and canopy of forest, but otherwise often down at lower levels in forest and forest edges, from sea level to 900m. Single birds and pairs are the normal unit, and nesting has been reported or is suspected from February through to August.

Black-headed Bulbul
■ *Microtarsus atriceps* 18cm

DESCRIPTION Both sexes bright olive-green, yellower on wings and tail, with black flight feathers, including black band on tail; tail-tip bright yellow, and head glossy blue-black, with contrasting pale eye. Juveniles duller than adults, with brown, non-contrasting head, usually easily identified by association with adults. **DISTRIBUTION** From NE India, through SW China, to Malaya Peninsula, Sumatra, Java, Borneo and Palawan. Resident in Peninsular Malaysia, Singapore, Sabah and Sarawak. **HABITAT AND HABITS** Found in forest and forest edges, flying in small flocks from tree to tree and over low scrub in disturbed areas such as old cultivation. Tail pattern easy to see in flight. Takes a wide variety of small fruits, and some insects.

Black-and-White Bulbul
■ *Microtarsus melanoleucos* 18cm

DESCRIPTION Overall glossy black; browner on head and vent, with large, clear white patch on lesser wing-coverts, crossed by a few black-tipped feathers. Black bill and feet. Female like male but less glossy black, and has smaller wing-patch. **DISTRIBUTION** Peninsular Malaysia, Sumatra and Borneo; resident. **HABITAT AND HABITS** Occurs from extreme lowlands in freshwater swamp forest and lowland forest, to uncertain elevations in hill forest. Among the three hill stations, only recorded in the past at lower elevations below Cameron Highlands. One of the least known bulbuls, in middle storey of tall, undisturbed forest. Thought to be nomadic, following fruit sources such as small figs.

Golden Babbler ■ *Cyanoderma chrysaeum* 12cm

DESCRIPTION Crown streaked black and yellow; brighter rufous-orange on forehead and above eye; plain brown on back, wings and tail. Below bright sullied yellow from chin to vent, with faint brownish streaking sometimes evident on flanks and lower breast. Sexes alike. **DISTRIBUTION** From Himalayas and S China, through Malay Peninsula, to Sumatra; resident. **HABITAT AND HABITS** Found from 900m upwards in hill, lower montane and upper montane forests. Occurs in pairs or small groups, frequently participating in mixed foraging flocks in lower storey. Common and characteristic species of all the hill stations. Song consists of about 10 notes in a series, with a distinct pause between the first and remaining notes.

Rufous-fronted Babbler
■ *Cyanoderma rufifrons* 12cm

DESCRIPTION Rather dull plumage, olive-brown above and olive-grey on sides of face and all of underparts; tinged buff on breast and undertail-coverts. Crown rufous, made distinct by pale eyebrow between crown and eye. Sexes alike; juveniles duller, paler, with less obvious brown crown than adults. **DISTRIBUTION** From mainland SE Asia, through Malay Peninsula, to Sumatra and Borneo; resident. **HABITAT AND HABITS** Found in hill and montane forests at about 800–1,500m. Scarcer than the Golden Babbler (see above), with a similar song but a less distinct pause after the first note. Tends to forage higher up in middle storey and above, singly or in pairs.

Sunda Scimitar Babbler

■ *Pomatorhinus bornensis* 19cm

DESCRIPTION Impressive rufous-chestnut flanks and back; throat, breast and centre of belly pure white; wings and tail dark brown. Head black with white eyebrow, and bill long, downcurved and bright yellow with black upper base. **DISTRIBUTION** Resident in southernmost Thailand and Peninsular Malaysia from 6° N, in Sumatra, Bangka and Borneo. Birds from Java and Bali previously included, as **Chestnut-backed Scimitar Babbler** *P. montanus.* **HABITAT AND HABITS** Found in middle storey and canopy of lowland evergreen rainforest, from extreme lowlands, up into lower montane forest to around 1,350m, the upper limit varying locally. Nests down in the understorey, in niche in earth bank or roadside cutting. Found singly or in pairs, using curved bill to probe for insects in bark, dead wood and epiphytes. Call a loud, fluty *Po hoi* or *Po hoi hoi.*

Large Scimitar Babbler ■ *Erythrogenys hypoleucos* 21cm

DESCRIPTION Large, dark brown above and whitish below, with heavy, pale grey, downturned bill. Crown and sides of face greyer; sides of neck, wings and tail warmer brown; underside white, with long white streaks margined darker against grey background of flanks and belly. **DISTRIBUTION** NE India, through Myanmar and N Thailand, to S China and Vietnam; discontinuously to Malay Peninsula; resident. **HABITAT AND HABITS** Occurs in the crowns of tall forest trees, in lower and tall upper montane forests. Seldom vocal, but vociferous once begun, giving three-note calls with head and neck stretched upwards, *HWIT tuo-wo!* possibly in a duet, with partner replying, *Tuo-wo-HUIT!* Found at Fraser's Hill, Cameron Highlands and Genting Highlands.

Grey-throated Babbler ■ *Stachyris nigriceps* 13cm

DESCRIPTION Dark brown back, wings and tail; more ochre-buff cheeks, breast and belly, with subdued pattern of white eyebrow and white malar patch imposed over grey crown; grey throat, and blackish around and in front of eye. **DISTRIBUTION** Resident from E Himalayas, through S China and continental SE Asia, to Peninsular Malaysia, Pulau Tioman, but not Singapore; and in Sumatra, Lingga, Natunas and Borneo. **HABITAT AND HABITS** Busy groups of 4–5 birds work through dense undergrowth, fern brakes and vegetation of forested roadsides and landslips, in lowland evergreen rainforest, and lower and upper montane forests, on slopes anywhere from just above sea level to beyond 2,000m; never in extreme lowlands over level ground. Continual tremulous, reeling trills between flock members. Insectivore, breeding in January–July.

White-headed Babbler ■ *Gampsorhynchus torquatus* 25cm

DESCRIPTION Light, bright rufous-brown, with white head, throat and underparts, warmly washed with buff on breast; irregular speckles between white head and warm brown back. Bill, eyes and feet all pale, with bill strongly hooked. **DISTRIBUTION** From

Myanmar and Thailand, discontinuously to Laos and Vietnam, and south to Malay Peninsula; resident. **HABITAT AND HABITS** Seldom seen, in hill forest and scrubby forest edges and bamboo, from about 250m upwards. Hill forest rather than montane species, seen for example at The Gap, but seldom present and may be rather nomadic. Small parties, possibly family groups, forage for insects among ferns and shrubs.

Moustached Babbler ■ *Malacopteron magnirostre* 17cm

DESCRIPTION Nondescript grey-brown above and off white below; browner on tail and with dark brown crown and dark moustache stripe; legs blue-grey. Juveniles duller than adults, with less contrasting moustache stripe. **DISTRIBUTION** From about 12° N in Myanmar, through Malay Peninsula, to Sumatra and Borneo; resident. **HABITAT AND HABITS** Found in lowland forest from nearly sea level to about 900m, in small parties or in pairs, sometimes in mixed foraging flocks with other species. Song is a series of about 3–6 spaced whistles, all on one pitch or slightly descending at the end. Gleans insects from foliage and may briefly chase flying insects. Known from The Gap below Fraser's Hill.

Rufous-winged Fulvetta ■ *Schoeniparus castaneceps* 12cm

DESCRIPTION Very small babbler, predominantly ashy-brown and white, with black-and-white face pattern. Broad white eyebrow curls behind dark ear-coverts, which are crossed by several dark-and-light bands, and dark chestnut crown is streaked with white. Black lesser wing-coverts, and edges of primaries form chestnut panel in wing. **DISTRIBUTION** E Himalayas from Nepal and Thailand, through to S China, discontinuously to Vietnam and south to Malay Peninsula; resident. **HABITAT AND HABITS** Occurs in lower and upper montane forests, where it frequents lower and middle storeys, and sometimes participates in mixed foraging flocks. Known from Fraser's Hill, Cameron Highlands and Genting Highlands.

Buff-breasted Babbler ■ *Trichastoma tickelli* 15cm

DESCRIPTION Somewhat undistinguished brown above, buff below; crown richer brown with faint streaking; pale throat. Sexes alike. **DISTRIBUTION** From easternmost

Himalayas to S China, south through mainland SE Asia, Indochina, to Malay Peninsula; resident. **HABITAT AND HABITS** Found in lower storey of undisturbed and lightly disturbed lower and upper montane forests, secondary growth and bamboo, in pairs and occasionally in mixed foraging flocks. Song is a monotonously repeated, two-note phrase, *wi-two*. Nest is a deep cup, sometimes fully roofed over with bamboo and other dry leaves.

Marbled Wren Babbler
■ *Turdinus marmoratus* 21cm

DESCRIPTION Rich chocolate-brown above, with narrow black scallops on crown and back; sides of face brighter rufous; dirty white patch in front of eye and white throat. Underparts blackish, with obscure white scallops fringing feathers. Tail rather long, and legs strong. **DISTRIBUTION** Mountains of Malay Peninsula and Sumatra; resident. **HABITAT AND HABITS** Elusive bird of tall, undisturbed forest in hills and mountains, from about the elevation of The Gap upwards, for example on side trails off the ascent road to Fraser's Hill; also Genting Highlands. Keeps to the ground, foraging in pairs in the leaf litter, turning over the litter and probing for insects. Song is a two-note whistle, the first pure high note hardly completed before the second (still higher) vibrating note is begun; delivered at a steady rate, about once per 3–5 seconds.

Streaked Wren Babbler ■ *Turdinus brevicaudatus* 14.5cm

DESCRIPTION Pale dusky-brown all over; more buff below, more grey-brown above, with entire underparts lightly streaked brown, and crown, back and rump lightly scaled black. **DISTRIBUTION** Resident from easternmost Himalayas and S Yunnan, through SE Asia, to mountains of Peninsular Malaysia, including Pulau Tioman but not Singapore. **HABITAT AND HABITS** Thai populations confined to lowland forest, but in northern Peninsular Malaysia and Pulau Tioman it is found on middle slopes, and further south it occurs in lower montane forest, at 750m to nearly 2,000m. Occurs on the ground, alone or in pairs, and utters loud, 2–4-note whistles. An insectivore, nesting on the ground, December–June.

Eyebrowed Wren Babbler ■ *Napothera epilepidota* 11cm

DESCRIPTION Very small and very short-tailed, with dark brown crown, back and wings; feathers streaked and wing-coverts have pale tips. Throat white, and underside light brown with pale streaks; white eyebrow, bordered above with black. **DISTRIBUTION** Mainland SE and E Asia, to Malay Peninsula, Sumatra, Borneo and Java; resident. **HABITAT AND HABITS** Found in forest in hills and mountains, from about the elevation of The Gap upwards; recorded at Fraser's Hill and Genting Highlands. Forages on the ground among the leaf litter, and hops from stem to stem among dense growth of plants or fallen twigs, usually remaining in pairs. Song is a short, penetrating, single pure whistle, given once every 3–4 seconds

Mountain Nun Babbler ■ *Alcippe peracensis* 15cm

DESCRIPTION Rounded grey head with neat, long, narrow black eyebrow; paler grey underparts and grey-brown back, wings and tail – virtually nondescript if eyebrow is not

noticed. **DISTRIBUTION** Hill forest in Indochina, discontinuously to mountains of Peninsular Malaysia; resident. **HABITAT AND HABITS** Found in middle and lower storeys of lower montane and upper montane forests, at 800–1,500m (occasionally 300–2,000m), including forest edges, old landslides and overgrown cultivation. Forages for invertebrates and some small fruits, and nests from January to May or June. Flamboyant song of 4–9 notes, varying across the scale, without which this species would be noticed much less often.

Cutia ■ *Cutia nipalensis* 18cm

DESCRIPTION Curiously like a nuthatch but with downcurved bill; white below, with flanks and lower breast strongly barred black. Sides of face maroon-brown; crown dark azure-blue. Wings dark; flight feathers have blue bases and white tips; tail dark with

black tip. In male back and rump are deep chestnut; in female olive-brown with black spots. **DISTRIBUTION** From Himalayas, discontinuously to Malay Peninsula; resident. **HABITAT AND HABITS** Found in lower and tall upper montane forests, keeping to larger trees. Creeps slowly along branches and trunks in middle storey, probing for insects among mosses, epiphytes and crevices in bark.

Chestnut-capped Laughingthrush ■ *Garrulax mitratus* 22cm

DESCRIPTION Bright rufous-chestnut cap and face, with white ring around eye and on forehead; otherwise entirely ashy-grey except for white wing-panel and chestnut vent and thighs. Borneo birds have buff mark only below eye (not entire ring), and slightly ochre tone to breast. Bill and legs bright orange-yellow. **DISTRIBUTION** Resident in mountains of Peninsular Malaysia, Sumatra and Borneo, including both Sabah and Sarawak. **HABITAT AND HABITS** Occurs at about 850–2,000m in lower and upper montane forests, from the canopy through middle and lower storeys of the forest, but rarely on the ground; in forest edges and secondary growth, including abandoned mountain cultivation and fern brakes. Call a repeated two-note whistle, breaking out into a great chorus among flock members. Nests around February–July.

Black Laughingthrush
■ *Garrulax lugubris* 26cm

DESCRIPTION Plumage entirely unglossed black, with blue bare skin behind eye and orange-yellow bill – perhaps redder in birds from Borneo, where adults (only) have bare greeny-yellow skin on crown and sides of neck. **DISTRIBUTION** Mountains of Peninsular Malaysia, Sumatra and Borneo, including both Sabah and Sarawak. **HABITAT AND HABITS** Insectivore found in middle and lower storeys of montane forest at 900–1,370m in peninsula, but highest record is 1,800m on Mt Kinabalu, Sabah. Occurs in pairs, often silent but wonderful when calling, a series of loud, frog-like gulps followed by rich, bubbling laughter. Bornean populations have been split by some authors, but similar calls, mutual responsiveness to tape recordings and scanty head feathering of peninsula birds make the split equivocal.

Chestnut-crowned Laughingthrush ■ *Trochalopteron erythrocephalum* 27cm

DESCRIPTION Rich chestnut cap, throat, breast and belly; face grey, and back grey-brown. Wing intricately patterned, with chestnut greater coverts, black primary coverts and golden fringes to flight feathers. **DISTRIBUTION** In 2007 suggested to be endemic

to mountains of Peninsular Malaysia, thus split off from closely related forms ('Chestnut-crowned Laughingthrush'), from Himalayas and S China, through Thailand and Indochina. **HABITAT AND HABITS** Found in understorey and middle interior of dark lower and upper montane forests, at 1,050–2,000m; occasionally ventures into old cultivation and edge vegetation. Usually in pairs, seldom larger groups, uttering cat-like mews and loud, jumbled whistling duets. Insectivore and partial frugivore, nesting mainly in January–April.

Long-tailed Sibia
■ *Heterophasia picaoides* 29–32cm

DESCRIPTION Smooth dark grey, paling on belly and undertail-coverts; white flash at base of wing feathers and white tips to long, graduated tail. Iris red; feet and slim bill black. **DISTRIBUTION** E Himalayan foothills to S Yunnan, discontinuously to Peninsular Malaysia and Sumatra. **HABITAT AND HABITS** Found at about 1,000–2,000m in lower and upper montane forests, frequenting crown and middle storey in small parties, including in mixed foraging flocks. Moves from tree to tree, quickly crossing open spaces at the hill stations, with long tail obvious in flight. Utters series of low notes as it feeds on insects and especially fruits, but produces no varied song. Nesting season in February–July is suggested.

Silver-eared Mesia ■ *Leiothrix argentauris* 17cm

DESCRIPTION Very colourful with black head, silvery-white ear-coverts, yellow forehead, nape, collar and breast, and yellow in wing. Wings otherwise grey with reddish bases to flight feathers; rump and undertail-coverts reddish in male, yellow in female.

DISTRIBUTION Resident from C Himalayan foothills, through S China, discontinuously to mountains of Peninsular Malaysia and Sumatra.
HABITAT AND HABITS Small, noisy parties surge through the understorey, giving a whistled eight-note song, *tee-oo-wit, tee-oo-wit, tee-oo*, and other varied notes. There are regional differences in the songs between populations in Southeast Asia. Found from the canopy of lower and upper montane forests, at 900–2,000m, and down into fern brakes and scrub in old cultivation.

Blue-winged Minla ■ *Siva cyanouroptera* 15cm

DESCRIPTION Entirely light grey above with white throat, underparts and sides of tail; light violet-blue sheen on wing feathers, often hard to see in dull misty conditions; pale iris distinctive. Female slightly duller than male.
DISTRIBUTION Resident from C Himalayan foothills, through S China, discontinuously through SE Asia to mountains of Peninsular Malaysia (not Singapore).
HABITAT AND HABITS Small flocks occur in the canopy and middle storey of lower and upper montane forests, at around 1,050–1,680m, passing through cultivated areas and clearings to forage in isolated big trees. Birds seek small insects among foliage, as well as taking small fruits.

Everett's White-eye ■ *Zosterops everetti* 11cm

DESCRIPTION Several white-eyes are tough to distinguish: green above, with grey flanks, and yellow throat and belly. This species has green (not yellow) forehead, uniform with rest of crown, and grey flanks and yellow of underside are richly coloured. **DISTRIBUTION** Patchily from N Thailand, through Malay Peninsula, to Borneo and

the Philippines; not in Sumatra and Java. Resident in Peninsular Malaysia, Sabah and Sarawak; absent from Singapore. **HABITAT AND HABITS** Found in hill and montane forests from a little above sea level to at least 1,700m, replacing the similar **Oriental White-eye** *Z. palpebrosa* (with yellow forehead) that occurs in coastal mangroves. Frequents the forest canopy in small, chittering flocks, flying from tree to tree, seeking small insects on foliage.

Yellow-browed Warbler ■ *Abrornis inornatus* 11cm

DESCRIPTION Subdued olive-green colour typical of leaf warblers; broad pale eyebrow bordered darker above and below, and two pale wing-bars on median and greater wing-coverts, as well as pale edges to

tertiaries. Lacks central crown-stripe of the Eastern Crowned Leaf Warbler (see opposite). Pale brown legs, and dark bill with little pale area near base of lower mandible. **DISTRIBUTION** N and NE Asia, wintering further south in E and SE Asia, to Malay Peninsula, with records in N Sumatra and Borneo; migrant in region. **HABITAT AND HABITS** In forest and particularly forest edges, a scarce migrant that has occurred at Fraser's Hill and Cameron Highlands. Call is a thin, high-pitched *suweep* given irregularly as it moves through the middle storey.

Eastern Crowned Leaf Warbler ■ *Seicercus coronatus* 12cm

DESCRIPTION Olive-green above, with broad pale eyebrow bordered darker; central pale stripe on rather dark crown, and single narrow but distinct wing-bar on greater coverts. Yellowish tone on vent. Orange legs and pale lower mandible. **DISTRIBUTION** NE and E Asia, wintering to mainland SE Asia as far as Malay Peninsula, Sumatra and W Java; migrant. **HABITAT AND HABITS** Can occur anywhere on passage, from lowlands to mountains, in middle and upper storeys of forest and secondary woodland.

Chestnut-crowned Leaf Warbler ■ *Seicercus castaniceps* 10cm

DESCRIPTION Chestnut central crown-stripe and eyebrows separated by black line, but sides of face, back and underparts are light grey, shading to pale yellowish on flanks and rump; two pale yellowish wing-bars. Sexes alike; juveniles duller than adults.

DISTRIBUTION Resident from C Himalayan foothills, through S China and SE Asia to Vietnam, and mountains of Peninsular Malaysia and Sumatra. **HABITAT AND HABITS** Found in lower montane forest at about 900–1,380m, and on mountains where the **Yellow-breasted Warbler** *Seicercus grammiceps* is absent (northern part of Main Range), extends to 1,800m; apparently the two species partially exclude each other. Nests under overhanging bank, predominantly in January–June.

Arctic Warbler
■ *Seicercus borealis* 13cm

DESCRIPTION Dusky-olive above, with pale brow narrowing behind eye, bordered dark below and no crown-stripe; single narrow wing-bar on greater coverts, and sometimes a faint one on middle coverts. White underparts washed grey. Flesh-coloured legs; dark bill with orange at base of lower mandible. **DISTRIBUTION** Across Palaearctic from Europe to E Asia, into Alaska; winters south to SE Asia, the Philippines and Indonesia; migrant in region. **HABITAT AND HABITS** Found in forest, forest edges and overgrown plantations, usually in the canopy of trees, foraging for insects. Occurs in lowlands and hills to 1,500m, and known from all three hill stations. Previously placed in the genus *Phylloscopus*.

Mountain Leaf Warbler ■ *Seicercus trivirgatus* 11.5cm

DESCRIPTION Small warbler, olive-green above and dirty yellow below, with central greenish crown-stripe bordered by wide black lateral crown-stripes, yellow brow and black line through eye; no wings-bars. **DISTRIBUTION** Resident in mountains of Peninsular Malaysia, Sumatra, Borneo, Java, Bali and the Philippines, to Lombok and Sumbawa. **HABITAT AND HABITS** Occurs in lower and upper montane forests at 1,300–2,160m in peninsula, and to 3,300m on Mt Kinabalu, Sabah. Pairs or small groups glean insects from foliage. Domed nest built in recess on banks or slopes, around February–April.

Bamboo Bush Warbler ■ *Abroscopus superciliaris* 9cm

DESCRIPTION Dark grey-brown crown and sides of face; greener back, wings and tail; whitish eyebrow and white breast; yellow lower breast to vent. Sexes alike; juveniles paler than adults, with less distinct brow and sides of face. **DISTRIBUTION** SE Asia, through Malay Peninsula, to Sumatra, Borneo, Java and Bali; resident. **HABITAT AND HABITS** Characteristic of bamboo in hilly forest at 500–1,500m, crossing the lowland/montane boundary, singly or in pairs or small parties. Often forages among bamboo, but also in other trees in middle storey. Now considered a bush warbler not a leaf warbler.

Mountain Tailorbird (Leaftoiler) ■ *Phyllergates cucullatus* 12cm

DESCRIPTION Green nape, back, wings and tail; white eyebrow, throat and breast merging into yellow belly. Tiny, with black line through eye and long, slim bill. Forehead and forecrown chestnut in adults, green in juveniles. **DISTRIBUTION** Resident from E Himalayan foothills, through S China, to Peninsular Malaysia, Sumatra, Borneo and Java, all the way to the Philippines and Lesser Sunda Islands. **HABITAT**

AND HABITS Found in lower and upper montane forests at 1,050–2,000m, in the understorey within the forest, but more typically at disturbed edges. Song is a roughly ascending series of five high notes, accompanied by buzzing from the other partner. The one 'tailorbird' that does not stitch leaves together to make its nest, a grassy pouch of dead leaves in tangled vegetation at the forest edge.

Pygmy Cupwing
■ *Pnoepyga pusilla* 9cm

DESCRIPTION Virtually tailless, tiny, rather upright bird of the forest floor; rich brown upperparts with buff spots on tips of wing-coverts. Sides of face washed rufous, and underparts thickly scalloped and scaled grey, brown and white. Sexes alike; juveniles plainer than adults, with less distinct spotting and scaling. **DISTRIBUTION** S, SE and E Asia, through Malay Peninsula, to Sumatra, Java and various Lesser Sunda Islands; resident. **HABITAT AND HABITS** Found in forest from 900m (about the elevation of The Gap) upwards and known from all three hill stations. Difficult to see well in dense understorey vegetation, foraging in the leaf litter. Call is a distinctive high-pitched, three-note whistle, *tee, too, tee*, the middle note the most powerful. There are variant notes, and several birds reply to each other and possibly duet.

Rufescent Prinia
■ *Prinia rufescens* 12cm

DESCRIPTION Grey head with short white brow and faint eye-ring; grey-brown back and tail with pale tips to tail feathers, and rufous tinge to wings. Underparts cream with no trace of yellow. Sexes alike; juveniles browner than adults. **DISTRIBUTION** Resident from E Himalayan foothills and parts of E India, through S China and SE Asia, to Peninsular Malaysia, but not reaching Singapore. **HABITAT AND HABITS** Occurs in rank grass and shrubs along forest edges, riverbanks and forested roadsides from extreme lowlands to a maximum of 1,500m in the mountains; characteristic of hilly areas and denser vegetation than the Yellow-bellied Prinia (see opposite). Pairs duet, one bird calling *chiep; chiep; chiep* while its partner gives a series of two- and three-note calls, *chir-chir, chir-chir-chir*. Nest like a tailorbird's, between stitched leaves in a bush.

Yellow-bellied Prinia

■ *Prinia flaviventris* 14cm

DESCRIPTION Grey head and ear-coverts with trace of pale eye-ring and short white brow (in female; obscure or absent in male); back and tail olive with white tips to tail feathers. Throat white, merging to light yellow on belly. Much variation, including feather wear and absence of yellow, causes continual confusion when using regional field guides. **DISTRIBUTION** Resident from Pakistan along Himalayan foothills, through S China to Taiwan, and through SE Asia to Peninsular Malaysia, Singapore, Sumatra, Nias, Borneo and Java. **HABITAT AND HABITS** Widespread throughout rural lowlands, in tall unkempt grassland, especially wet grassland with scattered shrubs, including patches of such habitat at forest and plantation edges. Presumed to be entirely insectivorous; males give a short rattling song, a cat-like mew of alarm, and a sputter of wingbeats that seems to be part of display.

Dark-necked Tailorbird ■ *Orthotomus atrogularis* 12cm

DESCRIPTION Green back, wings and tail, without pale eyebrow; entirely chestnut crown, grey sides of face, and throat with blackish streaks, faint in female but broad and coalescing in male; rest of underparts creamy-white. Note that the Common Tailorbird (see p. 122) can show black feather bases on its throat. **DISTRIBUTION** NE India and southernmost China, through SE Asia, to Singapore, Sumatra, the Anambas and Borneo. **HABITAT AND HABITS** Inhabits the canopy of forest from extreme lowlands to montane forest at 1,100m, and especially the understorey along logging tracks and forest edges, riverbanks and dense, tangled secondary growth to 1,400m or more. Utters a rising trill, repeated, and sometimes downturned. Nest is built within a one- or two-leaf stitched pouch.

Common Tailorbird ■ *Orthotomus sutorius* 12cm

DESCRIPTION Dark green wings, back and tail; chestnut cap, darker, duller and merging more smoothly into back than in the Dark-necked Tailorbird (see p. 121); light variable streaking on sides of face and throat. Always has chestnut thighs. Juveniles lack brown cap of adults, but usually have brownish tinge on forehead. **DISTRIBUTION** Indian subcontinent and Himalayan foothills, through S China and SE Asia, to Peninsular Malaysia, Singapore, Bintan and Java. **HABITAT AND HABITS** The most common garden tailorbird, but also widespread in cultivated areas, plantations, scrub, roadsides and riverbanks; originally confined to lowlands but has now extended to at least 1,700m with agricultural spread. Call a rapid, repeated *chik chik chik …* in monotonously prolonged bouts. Nest built within a one- to three-leaf stitched pouch, apparently in nearly every month.

Velvet-fronted Nuthatch ■ *Sitta frontalis* 13cm

DESCRIPTION Bright purplish-blue above and pearly-grey below, with bright red bill and feet. Black velvety stubble on forehead at base of bill, continuing backwards through eye, in male only, to nape; red eye-ring. **DISTRIBUTION** Resident from E Himalayan foothills, discontinuously through parts of India and Sri Lanka, to S China and SE Asia, and Peninsular Malaysia, Singapore, Sumatra, Borneo, Palawan and Java. **HABITAT AND HABITS** Occurs in pairs or often in small groups, including within mixed foraging flocks, in upper storey of tall evergreen rainforest from extreme lowlands to 1,150m in lower montane forest in peninsula, and even to 2,200m on Mt Kinabalu, Borneo (where the Blue Nuthatch, see below, is absent). Forages on large boughs. Nesting reported from February to June.

Blue Nuthatch ■ *Sitta azurea* 13cm

DESCRIPTION White chin, throat and upper breast sharply demarcated from rest of blackish head and belly; back, wings and tail increasingly blue towards rear, with bright blue edges to wing feathers. White iris and eye-ring. **DISTRIBUTION** Resident in mountains of very southernmost Peninsular Thailand, Peninsular Malaysia, Sumatra and Java. **HABITAT AND HABITS** Found in middle and upper storeys of lower and upper montane forests at around 900–1,960m, presumably displacing the Velvet-fronted Nuthatch (see above) from such altitudes in the peninsula. Occurs in pairs or small parties, foraging on trunks and boughs for a variety of invertebrates. Very little recorded about its breeding habits.

Common Myna ■ *Acridotheres tristis* 25cm

DESCRIPTION Smooth, plummy cinnamon-brown; head nearly black, with yellow bill and bare yellow skin around dark eye. White vent, large white wing-patch, and white tips to tail. In moult, some birds have entirely bare, scrawny yellow heads. **DISTRIBUTION** Resident from Middle East, through India and S China, to SE Asia, having invaded Peninsular Malaysia and Singapore during the past century, then Sumatra, and recently Sarawak, in small numbers. **HABITAT AND HABITS** At one time the most common myna in Peninsular Malaysia, associated with human agriculture and settlements, foraging on the ground, especially on short turf for grubs, and also taking fruits as well as rubbish from dumps. Forming communal roosts, often with crows, other starlings and mynas, numbers have been severely knocked back by invasion of the **Javan Myna** *A. javanicus*. Occurs patchily at Cameron Highlands, but not other hill stations.

Scaly Thrush ■ *Zoothera dauma* 30cm

DESCRIPTION Bulky yet elegant thrush with light olive-brown upperparts; underparts nearly white washed, with warm buff on upper breast; entire plumage scalloped with black. Folded wing shows pale tips to median wing-coverts, and in flight underwing is banded black and white. **DISTRIBUTION** C and E Palaearctic, wintering to S and SE Asia, to Malay Peninsula and Borneo; migrant or vagrant. **HABITAT AND HABITS** Rarely recorded, but easily overlooked as it feeds inconspicuously on the ground in dense vegetation in secondary growth; not deep in undisturbed forest, but can occur anywhere on migration and has been netted at Fraser's Hill.

Siberian Thrush
■ *Geokichla sibirica* 22cm

DESCRIPTION Male very dark, nearly black, with striking white eyebrow from behind bill nearly to nape. Darker males with little marking below tail are from Japan; slightly lighter grey males from mainland Asia have white tips to vent feathers. Female chocolate-brown above and on crown, rich rufous-buff below densely spotted buff, and with pale eyebrow and moustache streak. **DISTRIBUTION** E Palaearctic to Japan, wintering in SE Asia, through Malay Peninsula, to Sumatra, Java and Bali; migrant. **HABITAT AND HABITS** Arboreal, in forest and forest edges, usually in hilly terrain above elevation of The Gap, seeking fruits. Present at hill stations around September–March; numbers seldom large but varying between years.

Orange-headed Thrush ■ *Geokichla citrina* 21cm

DESCRIPTION Rich rufous-orange head and underparts, with back, wings and tail dark grey (in male) or olive-brown (in female), and white bar on bend of wing. There are significant variations in richness of orange plumage, whiteness or even presence of the wing-bar, and

of vertical dark bars on the face that are characteristic of juveniles. **DISTRIBUTION** S, SE and E Asia, wintering south to Malay Peninsula and Sumatra; migrant in region, with isolated resident populations in Sabah, Java and Bali. **HABITAT AND HABITS** Occurs on migration, and winters at any elevation from extreme lowlands upwards to limits of lower montane forest, in heavily shaded, closed canopy conditions. Forages on the ground, hopping forwards on the leaf litter in forests, parks and gardens, and recorded at Fraser's Hill and Cameron Highlands.

Eyebrowed Thrush ■

Turdus obscurus 22cm

DESCRIPTION Grey head, neck and upper breast; whitish eyebrow, and mark below eye, moustache and chin. Rufous breast and flanks; belly and vent white; upperparts brown. Adults have inconspicuous pale tips to wing-coverts, and female has a browner grey head than male. Juveniles have brown head and upperparts, and rufous underparts, spotted profusely buff and white. **DISTRIBUTION** C and E Palaearctic, wintering south to mainland E Asia and SE Asia, to the Philippines, Sulawesi and Lesser Sunda Islands; migrant in region. **HABITAT AND HABITS** Found in forest and tall tree plantations, at any elevation on migration, but characteristically wintering in hilly forest; one of the most common migrant thrushes at all three hill stations. Feeds in trees and on the ground, predominantly on fruits.

Oriental Magpie Robin ■ *Copsychus saularis* 20cm

DESCRIPTION Male has glossy black head, breast, back and wings, and white-sided tail. In Peninsular Malaysia, Singapore and Sarawak, birds have brilliant white belly, but Sabah males have entirely black belly. All have strong white wing-bar. Female more subdued grey and cream with wing-bar. **DISTRIBUTION** Resident in Indian subcontinent and southern third of China, through SE Asia, to Peninsular Malaysia, Singapore, Sumatra, Borneo, Java, Bali and most of the Philippines. **HABITAT AND HABITS** Garden bird par excellence, with a fine and varied song given by male or both sexes from orchard trees; also in plantations, secondary woodland and mangroves. Can invade edges of heavily logged forest next to cultivation, and forested riverbanks. Drops to the ground for insects, worms and small vertebrates, and breeds around January–June.

White-rumped Shama ■ *Kittacincla malabarica* Male 28cm; female 22cm

DESCRIPTION Blue-glossed black head, breast, back, wings and tail; rufous belly; white

rump and white edges to long tail. Female has same pattern as male, but is duller and shorter tailed; juveniles also have buff wing-spots. **DISTRIBUTION** Resident from C Himalayan foothills, patchily through Indian subcontinent and S China to Hainan, through Peninsular Malaysia, Singapore, Sumatra, Borneo and Java. **HABITAT AND HABITS** Found in understorey of lowland forest from sea level upwards, rarely to 1,200m in lower montane zone, including overgrown plantations and secondary woodland. Like Oriental Magpie Robins (see p. 127), persecuted by trapping because of fine, varied, sustained song. Nests in at least February–August; nest is a cup placed in any recess.

Dark-sided Flycatcher
■ *Muscicapa sibirica* 14cm

DESCRIPTION Dark grey-brown above; paler below with whitish throat, moustache and hint of collar; breast broadly streaked dark grey; short black bill; very narrow partial eye-ring and wing-bar may be present. Distinguished from the Asian Brown Flycatcher (see opposite) by shorter, all-black bill; heavier streaking on breast and flanks; lores hardly paler than rest of face; eye-ring still less visible. **DISTRIBUTION** From Himalayas, through mainland SE and E Asia, wintering south to Borneo, Sumatra and Java; migrant in region. **HABITAT AND HABITS** Found in tall forest and forest edges, wooded gardens and plantations, in lowlands to lower montane elevations. Sallies out from a twig perch to catch insects on the wing. Recorded from Fraser's Hill and Cameron Highlands.

Asian Brown Flycatcher ■ *Muscicapa latirostris* 13.5cm

DESCRIPTION Ashy-grey or grey-brown, with pale lores between bill and eye, and pale eye-ring; throat pale with no trace of extending backwards to form any collar; breast pale grey-brown, sometimes with faint streaks. Black feet, and yellow base to lower mandible. Plenty of plumage variation, but foot and bill colour and pale eye-ring are good features. The migrant **Brown-streaked Flycatcher** M. *williamsoni* has possibly been seen at Fraser's Hill, but the resident **Umber Flycatcher** M. *umbrosa* has not yet been recorded in highlands. **DISTRIBUTION** Resident through whole of NE Asia; and from Himalayas through S China and SE Asia to peninsular Thailand; migrant into Malay Peninsula, Borneo, the Philippines and Lesser Sunda Islands. Migrants occur throughout this region. **HABITAT AND HABITS** Single migrants perch on bare twigs of treetops, sallying out to snap up flies and mosquitoes, moths and other insects, at all the hill stations.

Ferruginous Flycatcher

■ *Muscicapa ferruginea* Male 12cm

DESCRIPTION Grey head, brown upperparts with more rufous panel on secondaries, and ferruginous breast and flanks below white throat. Rump and tail rufous, these and underparts making it the most readily identified of the small 'brown' flycatchers. Juveniles darker than adults, with buff streaks on crown, buff spots from back to rump, and dark streaks on breast. **DISTRIBUTION** From Himalayas to E Asia, wintering to SE Asia and the Philippines and Java; migrant in region. **HABITAT AND HABITS** Seen singly, perched on a conspicuous twig in middle or lower storey of forest edges, tree plantations and well-wooded parks. Often in hills but occurs down to sea level and up to the limits of lower montane forest; recorded at Fraser's Hill and Cameron Highlands.

Hill Blue Flycatcher

■ *Cyornis caerulatus* 15cm

DESCRIPTION Male deep blue above and orange-rufous below, shading gradually to pale belly and vent; no black at all on chin. Female brown above, slightly more rufous on wings and tail, and orange-rufous below, also shading steadily paler downwards like male. **DISTRIBUTION** From SW China, through Indochina and Malay Peninsula, to Borneo and Java. Resident in Peninsular Malaysia, Sabah and Sarawak; absent from Singapore. **HABITAT AND HABITS** Bird of hill forest from about 400m upwards, extending to about 1,200m in lower montane forest. Flycatches in middle and lower middle storeys of the forest, and usually seen singly. Distribution seems rather patchy; thought to be scarce in parts of Sabah but common in other forests at suitable altitudes

Pale Blue Flycatcher ■ *Cyornis unicolor* 17cm

DESCRIPTION Male powder-blue, paler and greyer on belly and vent. Female with rufous tail and uppertail-coverts; otherwise largely ashy-grey, white to pale grey on belly. The similar Asian Verditer Flycatcher (see p. 134) is more turquoise (both sexes), with brighter wings and lacking any grey on belly. **DISTRIBUTION** From NE India, through S China, to Malay Peninsula, Sumatra, Borneo and Java. Resident in Peninsular Malaysia, Sabah and Sarawak; absent from Singapore. **HABITAT AND HABITS** Found in forest and edges of forest clearings, in middle and upper storeys, often in lower hill slopes at about 200–900m, but recorded at extremes of nearly sea level to 1,400m. Rather inconspicuous but shows typical fly-catching behaviour from an exposed perch. Recorded from Cameron Highlands, but not the other hill stations.

Female

Male

Rufous-browed Flycatcher ■ *Anthipes solitaris* 12cm

DESCRIPTION Bright rufous-buff forehead, eyebrow, sides of face and ring around eye, contrasting with pure white chin and throat. Above olive-brown, more rufous tinge on wings, rump and tail; below olive-grey with buff tinge on breast. Sexes alike; juveniles streaked with rufous above, and with less contrasting rufous-buff on face and brow, and inconspicuous pale throat. **DISTRIBUTION** From Myanmar and mainland SE Asia, through Malay Peninsula to Sumatra; resident. **HABITAT AND HABITS** Occurs in montane forest above 800m, keeping largely to the understorey or even the ground, where it is fairly approachable. Nest built against a small bank on a slope. Alarm call is a harsh *churr*, and the song a series of several (three or typically more) thin, hesitant whistles.

Large Niltava

■ *Niltava grandis* 21cm

DESCRIPTION Large flycatcher, the male very deep dark violet, virtually black below, with brighter blue highlights on crown and sides of neck. Female rich dark brown, faintly streaked on face and upper breast, with bluish crown and blue patch on sides of neck. **DISTRIBUTION** Resident from C Himalayas, to Yunnan and uplands of SE Asia, to Peninsular Malaysia and Sumatra. **HABITAT AND HABITS** Seen singly or in pairs in lower, and less often upper, montane forests at 1,200–2,050m, often in mixed foraging flocks with other birds. Perches in middle storey and forest edges, sallying out to catch flying insects. Nesting estimated to occur in February–July.

Rufous-bellied Niltava ■ *Niltava sumatrana* 15cm

DESCRIPTION Similar to blue flycatchers in the genus *Cyornis*; deep purplish-blue upperparts with shining blue crown, carpals and rump; deep black face and throat; bright orange underparts. Female brown above, on face and throat, wings and tail, with grey crown, collar and breast, and small white crescent between brown throat and grey breast. **DISTRIBUTION** Mountains of Malay Peninsula and Sumatra; resident. **HABITAT AND HABITS** Seen in pairs in montane forest above about 1,500m in Peninsular Malaysia (apparently lower in Sumatra), so absent from Fraser's Hill, which is too low, but at Cameron Highlands it participates in mixed foraging flocks.

Blue-and-White Flycatcher

■ *Cyanoptila cyanomelana* 16cm

DESCRIPTION Deep blue above, without any purple tone; brighter blue crown; blackish face, throat and upper breast, sharply cut off to white lower breast and belly. Female soft grey-brown with more rufous edges to wing and tail feathers; pale below with light grey wash across breast, and pale rim around eye. **DISTRIBUTION** E and NE Asia, wintering south to Malay Peninsula, Borneo, Java, N Sulawesi and the Philippines; migrant in region. **HABITAT AND HABITS** Found in hill and lower montane forests above about 1,000m, often singly in forest edges or in fruiting shrubs such as *Melastoma* and *Medinilla*. Has been seen at Fraser's Hill and Cameron Highlands.

Asian Verditer Flycatcher
■ *Eumyias thalassinus* 16cm

DESCRIPTION Light blue-green all over, a little greener and a deeper colour than the Pale Blue Flycatcher (see p. 131), without any grey tone on belly. Female blue all over like male (therefore very unlike Pale Blue female), but black between bill and eye is reduced. **DISTRIBUTION** S, SE and E Asia, to Malay Peninsula, Sumatra and Borneo; resident. **HABITAT AND HABITS** Occurs in tall forest in lowlands and hills into lower montane forest, along forest edges, where it perches high up, singly or in pairs. Flies out to snatch flying insects, and also takes small fruits.

Lesser Shortwing
■ *Brachypteryx leucophris* 12cm

DESCRIPTION Two colour phases in male: rufous and slaty-blue. Rufous males warm brown above, paler brown on sides of face and below, with whitish throat and belly, and short, narrow white eyebrow in front of eye. Slate-coloured males dark grey above, mottled grey below, with white throat and belly, and white brow. Females similar to rufous males, but with less distinct white or buffy eyebrow. **DISTRIBUTION** Himalayas to E and SE Asia, to Sumatra, Java and Lesser Sunda Islands; resident. **HABITAT AND HABITS** Found in low growth or on the ground in montane forest from 900m upwards, often in pairs. Rich song lasts over two seconds, and is given at 10-second intervals, with a couple of slow introductory notes followed by a tumble of up-and-down whistles.

Rufous-headed Robin ■ *Larvivora ruficeps* 13cm

DESCRIPTION Male has grey back, wings and tail; grey below with whitish belly. Crown to nape bright orange-rufous, separated from brilliant white throat by black line through eye and sides of face. Tarsus and feet pale pink, slender and delicate. **DISTRIBUTION** Very small breeding range within Qinling Mountains, Sichuan and Shaanxi, SW China; migrant. **HABITAT AND HABITS** There are only three wintering records anywhere, in March 1963 at Cameron Highlands when a male was netted, one at Genting Highlands in April 2014 and one in Cambodia. On its breeding grounds occurs in temperate mixed forest and deciduous scrub, feeding on or near the ground, and Malaysian wintering records are in stunted montane forest.

Siberian Blue Robin ■ *Larvivora cyane* 14cm

DESCRIPTION Male greyish-blue above, pure white below, with sharp black cut-off between the two colours from bill to sides of breast. Female brown above washed with grey, bluer on rump and tail; underparts white, washed with buff on face, breast and flanks, with faintly mottled breast. **DISTRIBUTION** E Palaearctic, wintering through SE Asia, to Malay Peninsula, Sumatra, Borneo and rarely Java; migrant in region. **HABITAT AND HABITS** Found in understorey and particularly on the ground in lowland and hill forests, well up into montane elevations on migration. Forages among the leaf litter. Although widespread, among the hill stations it has been noted at Fraser's Hill but not yet at Cameron and Genting Highlands.

Chestnut-naped Forktail
■ *Enicurus ruficapillus* 20cm

DESCRIPTION White forehead and rich chestnut crown; black back (brown in female); black wings, long, forked tail and black throat, with white tail-edges and bars; white wing-bar and scaly white breast. Female duller than male; juveniles duller still. **DISTRIBUTION** Resident from 15° N in Thailand, southwards through Peninsular Malaysia, Sumatra and Borneo. **HABITAT AND HABITS** Found in lowland evergreen rainforest mainly on hill slopes to around 900m. First view is usually of a pied bird with a flash of chestnut, speeding away low over a rocky stream in the forest. Settles on rocks, especially near swirls around timber snags in water, and often cocks, fans and lowers tail. Call is a piercing whistle. Nests in rock cleft or bank, in most months of the year. Recorded below Cameron Highlands, but not listed for approaches to the other hill stations.

Slaty-backed Forktail
■ *Enicurus schistaceus* 23cm

DESCRIPTION Adults have black face below eye to throat, grey crown and mantle, and white rump; wings and tail black with white bars and tips to tail feathers, and underside white. Juveniles light brown above and paler scaly-brown below, with same wing and tail pattern. **DISTRIBUTION** From N India, through S China and Indochina, to Malay Peninsula. Resident in Peninsular Malaysia; absent from Singapore, Sabah and Sarawak. **HABITAT AND HABITS** Found in hilly and montane forests and forest edges, along small, rocky streams or wet roadsides in secluded areas, at about 600–1,300m in the region.

Malayan Whistling Thrush ■ *Myophonus robinsoni* 26cm

DESCRIPTION Difficult to distinguish from the Blue Whistling Thrush (see below), but smaller, more round headed, and with proportionately larger eye and more slender bill. Upper mandible black and lower one bright orange. Overall impression is neater, more compact and less sloppy about the tail, and less gangly about the neck and legs. Never shows pale spangles on tips of median wing-coverts. **DISTRIBUTION** Endemic to Peninsular Malaysia; resident. **HABITAT AND HABITS** Largely confined to ground level in montane forest. Once recorded from various hill stations and mountain peaks along Main Range, but has apparently declined, with few recent records from Cameron Highlands, leaving Fraser's Hill as the best opportunity to find it.

Blue Whistling Thrush

■ *Myophonus caeruleus* 32cm

DESCRIPTION Very big thrush, black all over with strong blue gloss; brighter blue spangles on wing-coverts, and (depending on race) on back and breast. Bill bright yellow, sometimes with black on upper mandible; feet grey. The Malayan Whistling Thrush (see above) is montane and lacks any speckling. **DISTRIBUTION** From C Asia southwards through S China, to SE Asia, Peninsular Malaysia (not south of 3° N), Sumatra and Java. **HABITAT AND HABITS** Resident around forested limestone outcrops in lowlands, where it feeds on large common snails, leaving conspicuous middens of broken shells. Nests in rock crevices, even within cave mouths. Dispersal away from limestone is limited, with records into nearby mangroves (for example Langkawi) along forested streams, locally at the lowland–montane transition, and recently found to be the the most common whistling thrush at Cameron Highlands. Call an intense single- to three-note whistle.

White-tailed Robin ■ *Myiomela leucura* 18cm

DESCRIPTION Male glossy black all over with blue highlights; brighter blue on crown and bend of wing, with broad tail often fanned, showing two white longitudinal panels. Female rich warm brown, paler on forehead and around eye, brighter rufous on secondaries, with similar tail pattern to male's. **DISTRIBUTION** C Himalayas eastwards to E China and Hainan, discontinuously through mainland SE Asia to Malay Peninsula; resident. **HABITAT AND HABITS** Found in montane forest above 1,200m, usually higher, foraging on the ground in the leaf litter or at a shady forested roadside, as well as low in understorey growth. Song consists of 6–7 high-pitched whistles packed into little more than a second, *u-weet-ohu- weet-uh*, the first note a little separate, the second and fifth notes emphasized and higher pitched than the rest.

Female

Male

Little Pied Flycatcher ■ *Ficedula westermanni* 11cm

DESCRIPTION Dumpy little flycatcher. Male black and grey, with very wide white eyebrow and long white wing-bar. Female grey-brown above and grey-white below, with dull rufous tail and narrow wing-bar. **DISTRIBUTION** Resident from W Himalayas, through S China, to Peninsular Malaysia (not Singapore), Sumatra, Java, Borneo, the Philippines, Sulawesi and Lesser Sunda Islands. **HABITAT AND HABITS** Seen alone or in pairs, in the crown of lower and upper montane forests and forest edges, at around 1,050–2,030m, but maximum of 3,100m on Mt Kinabalu. Gleans insects from foliage and also sallies out to catch passing insects in flight. Nests mostly in March to early June; nest a cup built among epiphytes or against an embankment.

Snowy-browed Flycatcher
■ *Ficedula hyperythra* 12cm

DESCRIPTION Male dark blue above, blacker on wings and tail, with orange throat gradually paling on breast and belly into white below tail, and with very short white eyebrow from forehead to just above eye. Female greyish-brown, with warmer brown edges to wing feathers, pale below washed with buff, and very short, pale buff brow reminiscent of male's. **DISTRIBUTION** From Himalayas, through E and SE Asia, as far as Sulawesi and Lesser Sunda Islands; resident. **HABITAT AND HABITS** Found in lower storey of montane forest, from about 1,200m upwards, usually alone or in pairs. Resident at all three of the hill stations.

Mugimaki Flycatcher ■ *Ficedula mugimaki* 13cm

DESCRIPTION Male blackish-grey with short white brow behind eye, and white wing-patch; rufous-orange below, shading gradually paler to belly and vent. Female greyish-brown above, with two narrow pale wing-bars, and light rufous-orange below, shading paler. **DISTRIBUTION** Cool temperate E Palaearctic, in Siberia and NE China, migrating south to Sundaland, the Philippines and Sulawesi. Migrant in Peninsular Malaysia, Singapore, Sabah and Sarawak. **HABITAT AND HABITS** Migrants have been seen from mangroves at sea level to more than 1,500m, in forests and forest edges, tall secondary woodland, parks and gardens. They perch in the middle and upper storeys of forest, and flycatch for insects.

Yellow-rumped Flycatcher ■ *Ficedula zanthopygia* 13cm

DESCRIPTION Male brilliant black and yellow with yellow rump. Distinguished from the male **Narcissus Flycatcher** *F. narcissina* by white (not yellow) brow and white wing-bar extending down secondaries. Female grey above and scaled buffy-white below, with white

wing-bar and yellow rump. **DISTRIBUTION** Resident in Siberia, Mongolia and China, migrating to Peninsular Malaysia, Singapore, Sumatra, Borneo and Java. **HABITAT AND HABITS** Found in edges of lowland evergreen forest and plantations, gardens and roadside trees, foraging for insects on foliage by perching, snatching or hovering. Bulk of arrivals from mid-September onwards, and most departures March–May, over-flying forest habitat. Usually solitary, foraging in the evenings. Was quite commonly netted at Fraser's Hill when migrating over mountains at night.

Pygmy Blue Flycatcher ■ *Ficedula hodgsoni* 10cm

DESCRIPTION Very small. Male dark blue above with black sides to face and bright blue forehead and eyebrow; underparts rufous-orange beginning from chin, fading to whitish at vent. Female olive-brown above and pale buff below, fading to white at vent; rump more reddish-brown than back and tail. **DISTRIBUTION** Himalayas and mainland SE Asia, discontinuously to Malay Peninsula, Sumatra and Borneo; resident. **HABITAT AND HABITS** Found in lower and upper montane forests at 850–900m upwards, in middle and lower storeys. Often occurs in pairs, flitting from perch to perch, and sometimes participates in mixed foraging flocks.

White-throated Rock Thrush ■ *Monticola gularis* 18cm

DESCRIPTION Male has bright blue crown and blue bend of wing, and dark brown back and wings scaled grey-brown, the wing with a single white bar; rump and underside from chin to vent brick-red, with white line down chin forming spot on centre of throat. Female like a half-sized version of **White's Thrush** *Zoothera aurea*, brown above spotted and scaled with black and buff; underparts pale buff scalloped with black; pale ring and backward line from eye. **DISTRIBUTION** NE Palaearctic from Russia to Korea and China, wintering south to Indochina and Thailand, rarely to Malay Peninsula. **HABITAT AND HABITS** Forest bird not frequenting rocky habitat, conceivably found anywhere on migration but seldom recorded, and netted as a night migrant at Fraser's Hill. When perched, tail is wagged up and down slowly, through a small angle. Feeds on insects, often on the ground.

Blue Rock-thrush ■ *Monticola solitarius* 22cm

DESCRIPTION Plain dark blue-grey, and during breeding season variable light and dark scale-like markings develop on body plumage. Migrant race has chestnut lower breast to vent. Female light uniform scaly-brown all over. **DISTRIBUTION** From the Mediterranean across temperate Europe and Asia, to Korea and Japan, south to Peninsular Malaysia and the Philippines; migrating to Africa, S and SE Asia, to Moluccas. Local resident in parts of Peninsular Malaysia; scarce migrant of Chestnut-bellied race in Peninsular Malaysia, Singapore, Sabah and Sarawak. **HABITAT AND HABITS** Residents most often near limestone and other cliffs; migrants anywhere but often near buildings, roadside cuttings, dams or other exposed faces, or near seashores.

Greater Green Leafbird ■ *Chloropsis sonnerati* 21cm

DESCRIPTION Male bright grass-green all over, with black throat-patch reaching eye where eyelid forms entirely black surround; superimposed blue moustache. Female has yellow throat,

light blue moustache, and yellow ring around eye; juvenile has yellow throat and separate yellow moustache. **DISTRIBUTION** Resident from about 15° N in Myanmar, through peninsular Thailand and Malaysia, to Singapore, Sumatra, the Natunas, Borneo and Java. **HABITAT AND HABITS** Found in lowland evergreen rainforest, peat-swamp forest, forest edges and spilling out to adjacent parkland. Feeds on soft fruits of second growth at forest edges, figs and possibly also nectar from flowers. Usually solitary or in pairs, sometimes joining mixed foraging flocks seeking insects. Song loud and quite attractive, imitating other species.

Lesser Green Leafbird ■ *Chloropsis cyanopogon* 18cm

DESCRIPTION Tough to distinguish; male's throat-patch tends to be outlined faintly with yellow; bill is proportionately smaller than Greater Green Leafbird's (see opposite), and black does not completely surround eye. Female has green throat, blue moustache and no blue in wing. **DISTRIBUTION** Resident from nearly 12° N in Myanmar, through peninsular Thailand and Malaysia, to Singapore, Sumatra and Borneo. **HABITAT AND HABITS** Behaviour very much like Greater Green's, in the crowns of trees in lowland evergreen rainforest, secondary forest and forest edges, and it is about as common, from the extreme lowlands extending just into montane forest at around 1,100m. Takes various fruits and figs, possibly nectar, and invertebrates while in mixed foraging flocks. Attractive warbling song, but nesting is little known.

Orange-bellied Leafbird ■ *Chloropsis hardwickii* 19cm

DESCRIPTION Bright sage-green above and subtle orange below, with black sides of face and throat, and long, purplish-black panel along wing. Female grass-green with orange flush on lower belly and undertail-coverts; limited blue on wing-coverts and inner secondaries. **DISTRIBUTION** Resident from W Himalayan foothills, through S China to Hainan, and SE Asia to mountains of Peninsular Malaysia. **HABITAT AND HABITS** In region, only found in montane forest, at about 900–1,900m, in the canopy and middle storey of upper and lower montane vegetation and along forested roadsides; occasionally down to 820m in hill forest. Male and female both sing, a wide range of beautiful notes including imitations of other species. Nesting surprisingly unknown, considering that the hill stations are so well visited by birdwatchers.

Blue-winged Leafbird ■ *Chloropsis cochinchinensis* 18cm

DESCRIPTION Bright grass-green, the male with black throat-patch, yellow flush over most of head, blue flash on carpel and down edge of wing, and bluish tail. Female has green throat and blue moustache like the female Lesser Green Leafbird (see p. 143), but distinct blue flash at edge of wing. **DISTRIBUTION** Resident from NE India to S China and SE Asia, through Peninsular Malaysia, Singapore (at least some introduced), Sumatra, the Natunas, Borneo and Java. **HABITAT AND HABITS** Found at edges of lowland evergreen rainforest, and sometimes also the canopy, as well as peat-swamp forest and secondary woodland, from extreme lowlands to about 1,250m. Consumes very wide range of fruits and invertebrates. Song is a series of squeaky chirps, rather irregular and varied, the notes spaced out.

Asian Fairy Bluebird

■ *Irena puella* 25cm

DESCRIPTION Male black on most of face, throat and underparts; largely black wings; crown, back, inner wing-coverts, rump, vent and tail-coverts brilliant glossy sky-blue. Female deep, dark powder-blue all over. Both sexes have reddish eyes and are quite bulky. **DISTRIBUTION** Resident from C Himalayas, through much of India and Sri Lanka, southernmost China and SE Asia, to Peninsular Malaysia, Singapore, Sumatra, Borneo, Java and Palawan. **HABITAT AND HABITS** Occurs in the canopy and middle storey of lowland evergreen rainforest, peat-swamp forest and secondary woodland, and less often at high altitudes into lower and even stunted upper montane forest to 1,900m. Takes many species of fruit and invertebrate, often snatching food while in flight, and seen singly or in pairs except at major fig and fruit trees, where numbers can gather. Song much less varied and prolonged than that of leafbirds. Nests around February–June.

Yellow-breasted Flowerpecker ■ *Prionochilus maculatus* 9cm

DESCRIPTION Dark olive-green above. White moustache and white chin separated by dark malar stripe; rest of underparts bright yellow with strong olive-green streaks, leaving central band of unmarked yellow down breast. Inconspicuous crown-spot fiery orange in male, dull ochre in female. **DISTRIBUTION** Resident from about 13° N in peninsular Thailand, through Malaysia to Singapore (past resident and possible dispersant), Sumatra, Bunguran and Borneo. **HABITAT AND HABITS** Common in middle and lower storeys of lowland evergreen rainforests from extreme lowlands to about 900m, sparse in lower montane forest to 1,250m in Sabah and Sarawak, and to 1,500m in Peninsular Malaysia. Arboreal foliage-gleaning insectivore and partial frugivore, usually seen alone.

Scarlet-breasted Flowerpecker ■ *Prionochilus thoracicus* 10cm

DESCRIPTION Male's head black, with black band across breast enclosing large, bright orange-red patch; red spot on crown; back olive-green; lower breast and belly olive-yellow; wings and tail black. Female olive-green above; orange-yellow below, fading to grey on belly; head grey with paler stripes on moustache and chin. **DISTRIBUTION** Malay Peninsula, Sumatra and Borneo; resident. **HABITAT AND HABITS** Found in lowland and peat-swamp forest; scarce and patchy in hilly forest to above the montane forest transition. Easily overlooked in the forest canopy, but will come lower at forest edges and has been recorded on the approaches to Fraser's Hill.

Crimson-breasted Flowerpecker ■ *Prionochilus percussus* 10cm

DESCRIPTION Male grey-blue above from forehead to tail, including sides of face and wings; bright yellow below, paler on throat and vent, with scarlet-orange patch in centre-line of breast. Red patch on crown, and white moustache edged below with grey-blue. Female greyish-olive, paler and greyer below, with yellowish centre-line of breast and belly; obscure orange crown-patch and white moustache. **DISTRIBUTION** Malay Peninsula, Sumatra, Borneo and Java; resident. **HABITAT AND HABITS** Usually found in forest edges, in lowlands to about 1,000m, often feeding in roadside shrubs such as *Melastoma malabathricum*, taking soft fruits. Seen singly or in pairs, keeping fairly low down.

Yellow-vented Flowerpecker ■ *Dicaeum chrysorrheum* 10cm

DESCRIPTION Olive-brown above, with white spot in front of eye; underparts white, heavily streaked with black from throat to belly; vent sulphur-yellow. Sexes alike but juveniles duller than adults, with greyer streaking on underparts. **DISTRIBUTION** From Himalayas and mainland SE Asia, to Malay Peninsula, Sumatra, Borneo, Java and Bali; resident. **HABITAT AND HABITS** Occurs in lowland and hill forests, occasionally reaching montane elevations as at Fraser's Hill and Genting Highlands. Often seen singly, frequenting the upper storey, and sometimes participating in mixed foraging flocks.

Thick-billed Flowerpecker ■ *Dicaeum agile* 10cm

DESCRIPTION Rather nondescript grey-brown, but with poorly defined pale spot in front of eye, pale moustache streak and pale underside with ill-defined grey streaking. Frequent side-to-side tail wagging and white tail-spots distinguish it from the lowland **Brown-backed Flowerpecker** *D. everetti* (not recorded at hill stations). **DISTRIBUTION** S and SE Asia, to Malay Peninsula, Sumatra, Java and Bali, Borneo and the Philippines; resident. **HABITAT AND HABITS** Found in the canopy of tall undisturbed and logged forest, in lowlands, hills, and hill dipterocarp forests. Often seen alone, but occasionally in groups visiting fruiting trees.

Orange-bellied Flowerpecker ■ *Dicaeum trigonostigmum* 8cm

DESCRIPTION Slaty-blue head, upper breast, back, wings and tail, and grey throat; brilliant orange lower breast to vent, and orange-yellow lower back and rump. Female olive-grey, unstreaked, with creamy-yellow rump and centre to belly. **DISTRIBUTION** Resident from Bangladesh, through peninsular Thailand and Malaysia, to Singapore, Sumatra, Borneo, the Philippines, Java and Bali. **HABITAT AND HABITS** Found in edges of lowland evergreen rainforest from sea level upwards into montane habitats with a typical

maximum of 1,200m, exceptionally 1,650m in Sarawak. Also enters tall plantations, well-wooded parkland, logged forest, and occasionally mangroves and peat-swamp forest. Feeds on varied small fruits, including those of mistletoes, plus insects and nectar. Nest is a hanging pouch in the understorey, with records over a wide scatter of months.

Plain Flowerpecker ■ *Dicaeum minullum* 8cm

DESCRIPTION Tiny, nondescript olive-brown bird with green wash on crown and upperparts, paler and greyer below, with pale lores between bill and eye. Bill short, slender and downcurved. **DISTRIBUTION** From Himalayas through mainland SE Asia, to Malay Peninsula, Sumatra, Borneo and Java; resident. **HABITAT AND HABITS** Found in lowland forest and forest edges, feeding on nectar and fruits of epiphytic mistletoes and other soft berries. Occurs uphill into lower montane elevations, and has been recorded on the approaches to Fraser's Hill.

Scarlet-backed Flowerpecker ■ *Dicaeum cruentatum* 8cm

DESCRIPTION Male has a broad scarlet line all the way from forehead over crown and down back to rump; white band from throat down centre of breast to vent; black sides of face, wings and tail; grey flanks. Female olive-grey, with broader creamy band from throat to vent, and red rump. **DISTRIBUTION** Resident from E Himalayas, through S China and SE Asia, to Peninsular Malaysia, Singapore, Sumatra, Riau and Borneo. **HABITAT AND HABITS** One of the most often seen flowerpeckers, in tall secondary growth, orchards, tree plantations and parkland, usually singly; also along edges of lowland evergreen and peat-swamp forest to a maximum of 870m. Soft fruits, nibbled to pieces if too big to swallow, mistletoes and soft-bodied invertebrates are eaten. Breeding reported in November–August.

Fire-breasted Flowerpecker
■ *Dicaeum ignipectus* 8cm

DESCRIPTION Male has slaty upperparts from forehead to tail, with blue-green gloss especially on crown and wings; dirty buff underparts with red splash on upper breast and black central streak on lower breast. Female light olive, greyer on head, buff below and with dark tail. DISTRIBUTION From Himalayas, through E and SE Asia, to Malay Peninsula, Sumatra and the Philippines; resident. HABITAT AND HABITS Found in forest, forest edges, shrubs and grass clearings in old cultivation; largely confined to hilly areas above 900m. Recorded at all three hill stations, feeding on soft fruits such as figs and mistletoe berries.

Ruby-cheeked Sunbird ■ *Chalcoparia singalensis* 11cm

DESCRIPTION Male glossy dark green above and rich yellow below, with orange suffusion on throat and upper breast, and red sides of face. Female olive-green above with grey tone to head; yellow below with light orange suffusion on throat and upper breast.

DISTRIBUTION From Himalayas, through mainland SE Asia, to Malay Peninsula, Sumatra, Borneo and Java. HABITAT AND HABITS Inhabits lowland forest to about 1,000m, just into montane elevations. Frequents mostly middle and upper storeys, and is therefore less obtrusive than Black-throated and Temminck's Sunbirds (see opposite and p. 152). Recorded from below Fraser's Hill.

Plain Sunbird ■ *Anthreptes simplex* 12cm

DESCRIPTION Entirely olive-green with slightly greyer head, grey throat and yellowish-grey underparts. Male has small iridescent patch of dark purple on forehead, absent in female. **DISTRIBUTION** Malay Peninsula, Sumatra, Borneo and various offshore islands; resident. **HABITAT AND HABITS** Occurs in forest and forest edges in lowlands and hills, reaching lower montane elevations and recorded from below Fraser's Hill. Found in high scrub, along forest edges, in *Macaranga*, *Saurauia* and other fruiting trees, sometimes with mixed foraging flocks.

Black-throated Sunbird ■ *Aethopyga saturata* Male 15cm; female 11cm

DESCRIPTION Male overall very dark with yellow rump and long central tail feathers; head iridescent blue-black; breast and back maroon; belly grey. Female olive-grey with pale yellow rump and grey throat. **DISTRIBUTION** Resident from C Himalayas, through S China, and discontinuously in SE Asian highlands to Peninsular Malaysia. **HABITAT AND HABITS** Found at 820–2,000m, from the canopy to lower storey and edges of lower and upper montane forest, including stunted forest on ridgetops. Seen singly or in pairs, often in mixed foraging flocks, taking tiny invertebrates, and nectar from tubular flowers of forest epiphytes, as well as from garden flowers and weeds. Breeding implied over a wide range of months.

Temminck's Sunbird

■ *Aethopyga temminckii* 10–12.5cm

DESCRIPTION Brilliant scarlet with yellow rump and scarlet tail. Lower breast and belly off white; on face two violet moustache stripes and two crown stripes join over nape. Black wings with red coverts. Female olive-grey with rufous sides to base of tail, and faintly rufous fringes to wing feathers; rump plain. **DISTRIBUTION** Resident from about 8° 30' N in peninsular Thailand and Malaysia (but not Singapore), to Sumatra and Borneo. **HABITAT AND HABITS** Found in middle and lower storeys of lowland evergreen rainforest, from extreme lowlands to 300m, exceptionally to 1,200m in the peninsula, and 1,650m in Sarawak and Sabah. Usually solitary or in pairs, taking nectar from a variety of forest epiphytes, rhododendrons and introduced flowers, and eating various small insects. Formerly called the Scarlet Sunbird, the name now reserved for the species in Java.

Thick-billed Spiderhunter ■ *Arachnothera crassirostris* 17cm

DESCRIPTION Dark olive-green on head and upperparts; paler olive-grey below; yellower on lower breast and belly, with pale feathering above and below eye forming incomplete eye-ring. The Little Spiderhunter (see opposite) also has pale markings above and below eye, but has a greyer head and colder, whiter face and throat, and grey moustache line. **DISTRIBUTION** Malay Peninsula, Sumatra and offshore islands, and Borneo; resident. **HABITAT AND HABITS** Found in forest, forest edges and adjacent plantations, in lowlands and hills into lower montane elevations. Keeps largely to middle and upper storeys. Recorded on the approaches to Fraser's Hill and Cameron Highlands.

Long-billed Spiderhunter ■ *Arachnothera robusta* 21cm

DESCRIPTION Muted and featureless olive-green head; dark olive-green on back and wings; yellowish below, particularly on belly, with faintly streaked breast. Tail with pale tips to feathers visible on underside. Bill black and impressively long and curved. **DISTRIBUTION** Malay Peninsula, Sumatra, Java and Borneo; resident. **HABITAT AND HABITS** Found in lowlands, hills and lower montane forest to 1,300m; most common towards upper end of this range of elevations. Usually

feeds high in the forest canopy, often perched on bare twigs, and protects nectar sources aggressively. Recorded on the approaches to Fraser's Hill and Cameron Highlands.

Little Spiderhunter ■ *Arachnothera longirostra* 16cm

DESCRIPTION Face and upper breast grey, shading to yellow belly; narrow dark moustache bordering pale sides of face; crown scaly dark grey, leading to olive wings and tail. Orange tuft can be revealed at bend of wing. **DISTRIBUTION** Resident in Himalayas and India, through S China and SE Asia, to Peninsular Malaysia, Singapore, Sumatra, Borneo, Java, and C and S Philippines. **HABITAT AND HABITS** Among the most common birds of the understorey in logged and unlogged lowland evergreen rainforests, from extreme lowlands into montane forest at 1,680m. Lively and often noisy, with an endlessly repeated chip when perched, or singly when in flight. Typically associated with wild banana, whose flowers are a major source of nectar; also invertebrates.

Yellow-eared Spiderhunter ■ *Arachnothera chrysogenys* 18cm

DESCRIPTION Dark olive-green spiderhunter, slightly smaller than the Spectacled Spiderhunter (see opposite), with breast and belly faintly streaked, reaching to yellow

thighs; bright yellow but often incomplete eye-ring that typically does not touch large yellow cheek-patch. Juveniles duller than adults, especially eye-ring and cheek-patch. **DISTRIBUTION** Resident from about 13° N in Thailand, through Peninsular Malaysia and Singapore, Sumatra, Riau, Borneo and Java. **HABITAT AND HABITS** Flowers of epiphytes and of canopy trees provide most food in the lowland evergreen rainforest, from sea level upwards; at least visits montane forest to a maximum record of 2,010m. Also in logged forest and tree plantations, and visits roadside trees such as *Erythrina*. Call reportedly higher pitched than that of Spectacled, but very similar plumage has led to confusion over their habitats and breeding records.

Streaked Spiderhunter
■ *Arachnothera magna* 18cm

DESCRIPTION Olive-green above from forehead to tail, and buffy-white below from chin to vent, the entire plumage finely streaked blackish; bright orange-yellow feet often clearly visible. **DISTRIBUTION** Resident from C Himalayan foothills, through S China and highland SE Asia, to Peninsular Malaysia. **HABITAT AND HABITS** Characteristic bird of lower and upper montane forests in the peninsula, at around 800–1,800m, in middle and upper storeys, and in roadside vegetation at the hill stations. Takes nectar from banana flowers at forest edges, and insects from tangles of epiphytes and lichen on branches. Quick, single alarm notes and two-note flight call can often be heard. Nesting remarkably under-recorded, considering the species is fairly common.

Spectacled Spiderhunter ■ *Arachnothera flavigaster* 21cm

DESCRIPTION Quite a bulky spiderhunter, overall olive-green, greyer on breast and yellower on belly, with distinct yellow ring around eye, the ring complete and linked with yellow patch on ear-coverts. DISTRIBUTION Malay Peninsula, Sumatra and Borneo; resident. HABITAT AND HABITS Found in logged forest and secondary growth, and coconut and other tree plantations, often at lower level in trees than the otherwise similar Yellow-eared Spiderhunter (see opposite). Takes nectar from a variety of cultivated and forest trees, often aggressively protecting nectar sources against interlopers.

Grey-breasted Spiderhunter ■ *Arachnothera modesta* 17cm

DESCRIPTION Dull olive-green upperparts, whitish-grey underparts; crown and entire underparts narrowly streaked with grey. Much less heavily streaked than the Streaked Spiderhunter (see opposite), and no yellow on face or underparts. DISTRIBUTION Malay Peninsula, Sumatra and Borneo (except Sabah); resident. HABITAT AND HABITS Found in undisturbed and logged lowland forests, to about the elevation of The Gap; not yet recorded on approaches to the other hill stations. Confined to the understorey, and less common than the Little Spiderhunter (see p. 153). Feeds at flowers of wild banana and gingers. Research is needed on the status of spiderhunters resembling Grey-breasted at higher elevations.

Purple-naped Spiderhunter ■ *Arachnothera hypogrammica* 15cm

DESCRIPTION Short-billed spiderhunter more resembling sunbirds, except that it is

predominantly deep olive-green above and below. Breast heavily streaked blackish from chin to lower breast, more heavily in male than in female, and male has shining purple nape-patch and rump. **DISTRIBUTION** Mainland SE Asia, to Malay Peninsula, Sumatra and Borneo; resident. **HABITAT AND HABITS** Found in lower and middle storeys of tall forest in lowlands and hills, extending into hill dipterocarp forest. Has been recorded on the approaches to Fraser's Hill, but not yet at the other hill stations.

Pin-tailed Parrotfinch ■ *Erythrura prasina* Male 15cm; female 12cm

DESCRIPTION Male has blue face, green crown, back and wings, and red rump and long pointed tail. Below blue throat, underparts are fawn with red centre to belly. Female

similar to male but less brightly coloured, with shorter tail and no red on belly. **DISTRIBUTION** SE Asia, to Malay Peninsula, Sumatra, Java and Borneo; resident but mobile. **HABITAT AND HABITS** Parrotfinches are adapted to exploit bamboos that produce seeds en masse over large areas. They are therefore seen only occasionally but can gather in big numbers when food is abundant in one area. Found in hill forest, old secondary growth over landslides and forest edges. Recorded from The Gap at Fraser's Hill and below Genting Highlands.

Tawny-breasted Parrotfinch ■ *Erythrura hyperythra* 10cm

DESCRIPTION Blue restricted to forehead; green crown, back and wings; buff face, underparts and rump. Blue forehead more extensive, and buff face and throat richer tawny, in male than in female. **DISTRIBUTION** Limited to small montane areas in Malay Peninsula and Borneo, and in Sulawesi, Java, Bali and Lesser Sunda Islands; resident. **HABITAT AND HABITS** Unpredictable occurrence in montane forest and forest edges. Its requirements and differences from the Pin-tailed Parrotfinch (see opposite) are not well understood, but it never forms the rare, big aggregations once seen in that species. Known from Cameron Highlands.

White-rumped Munia ■ *Lonchura striata* 12cm

DESCRIPTION Blackish-brown, with crown and back very finely streaked pale; face and upper breast, and upper and lower tail-coverts, paler brown; lower breast and belly as well as rump dirty white. Tail feathers slightly pointed. **DISTRIBUTION** S, SE and E Asia, to Malay Peninsula and Borneo; resident. **HABITAT AND HABITS** Found from lowlands to montane elevations, usually in hilly country, in grassland with scattered woodland, along forest edges and secondary growth. Occurs in small flocks or pairs. Recorded at all the hill stations.

Scaly-breasted Munia ■ *Lonchura punctulata* 10cm

DESCRIPTION Head, throat, back and wings chestnut, darkest around face; breast and belly white strongly scalloped with black, the scallops extending to rump. Juveniles sandy-brown all over like most munias, and best identified by association with adults. **DISTRIBUTION** Resident from Himalayas, through S China and SE Asia, to Lesser Sunda Islands; introduced to various tropical areas. In Peninsular Malaysia, Singapore and since 1993 Sabah, where it is spreading. **HABITAT AND HABITS** Munia associated with human cultivation, especially paddy fields, grassland, old mining land and suburban areas. Eats many types of grass seed, as well as ripening rice, and big flocks can build up. Nest is a grassy oval in dense vegetation, with records nearly throughout the year, and fewest in rainy season.

Eurasian Tree-sparrow ■ *Passer montanus* 14cm

DESCRIPTION Chestnut cap and small black bib, separated by grey-white cheeks with black spot on ear-coverts. Back and wing-coverts streaky brown with black-and-white streaks and wing-bar; underside buffy-grey. Sexes alike; juveniles merely duller. **DISTRIBUTION** Discontinuously from Europe, through C Asia to Japan, south to the

Philippines and Indonesia, and throughout our area. **HABITAT AND HABITS** Commonly associated with towns, villages, factories and ports, often in large flocks, feeding on short-grass areas, on pavements and in roadside bushes; also in rural habitat to a maximum of 1,400m within the area. After initial colonization, populations tend to decline again if habitat is too well managed, especially where nesting opportunities are lost in crevices and roofs of old buildings. Eats grass seeds, spilt food and any tiny fragments picked from the ground, with feeding by day and by night in brightly lit places.

Forest Wagtail ■ *Dendronanthus indicus* 17cm

DESCRIPTION Grey-brown crown, face, back, rump and tail; white eyebrow; white underparts with two strong blackish (sometimes incomplete) bands across breast. Wings have two black and two white bars, very obvious in flight or when perched. **DISTRIBUTION** NE and E Asia, wintering to Himalayas, E and SE Asia, to Sumatra, Java and Bali; migrant in region. **HABITAT AND HABITS** Found in wooded countryside, foraging mostly on the ground and flushing into dense

vegetation, where it sometimes perches. Usual tail-wagging motion is from side to side, not up and down. Known from Fraser's Hill, and should occur at the other hill stations.

Grey Wagtail ■ *Motacilla cinerea* 19cm

DESCRIPTION Slim, with long tail bobbed up and down; grey back, darker grey crown and sides of face with white brow; pale yellowish beneath leading to yellow vent, with white sides of tail. In flight, white wing-bar and yellow rump are visible. **DISTRIBUTION** From North Africa, through Europe and Asia to Japan, migrating south to Africa, India and SE Asia to N Australia. Migrant in Peninsular Malaysia, Singapore, Sabah and Sarawak. **HABITAT AND HABITS** Typically seen singly on the ground, on unfrequented roads, logging tracks and especially near streams. Trots after small insects and other invertebrates on surfaces of rocks, at the water's edge or even on wet tarmac, with tail wagging intermittently, at any altitude from sea level to mountains. Two-syllable call given when taking flight.

White Wagtail ■ *Motacilla alba* 18cm

DESCRIPTION Slim grey, black and white bird with long tail incessantly wagged up and down. White face with blackish crown, black line through eye, and black bib from throat to upper breast; rest of upperparts grey or blackish, underparts white washed with grey. Extensive white wing-bar and white outer tail feathers conspicuous in flight.

DISTRIBUTION Various races across the Palaearctic, wintering to S, E and SE Asia, south to Malay Peninsula, Sumatra and Borneo, where it is a scarce migrant. **HABITAT AND HABITS** Found in open environments from the coast to inland, at higher elevations when on migration, and known from Fraser's Hill. Feeds on the ground, teetering along, continually changing direction to snap up tiny insects.

Olive-backed Pipit ■ *Anthus hodgsoni* 16cm

DESCRIPTION Dark olive back, wings and tail, without white 'braces' on back; whitish below with buff wash and heavy black streaking; pale brow, small, pale spot on ear-coverts, and black streaks forming mesial streak that encloses pale moustache below ear-coverts. **DISTRIBUTION** E Palaearctic, from Himalayas to E Asia, wintering south to Malay Peninsula, Borneo and the Philippines; migrant in region. **HABITAT AND HABITS** Found in forest, tree plantations and coastal vegetation, foraging on the ground but flushing into the middle and upper canopies. Even when wintering, occasionally gives short, towering display flights from tops of trees. Primarily in lowlands, but migrants recorded at all three hill stations.

Paddyfield Pipit ■ *Anthus rufulus* 16cm

DESCRIPTION Fairly slim, upright pipit present all year. Well-spotted breast. Typically gives three-note *tchep tchep tchep* flight call when disturbed. Very similar **Richard's Pipit** *A. richardi* is bigger, less heavily spotted, typically utters a one-note *shreep* and is present only as a wintering bird. **DISTRIBUTION** India and S China, through Indo-Malaya, to Peninsular Malaysia, Singapore, Sumatra, Borneo, Java, the Philippines and Lesser Sunda Islands. **HABITAT AND HABITS** Occurs on short grass like that at airfields and golf courses, often with wagtails, foraging for small insects such as flies and grasshoppers, and spiders. Trots forwards and draws itself upright on halting, often on a tussock or soil clod. Nest well hidden among grass, and very tough to locate.

Brown Bullfinch ■ *Pyrrhula nipalensis* 17cm

DESCRIPTION Ashy grey-brown head, back and underparts, becoming paler on belly, with base of bill (forehead, lores) to eye outlined in black. Wings and rather long tail glossy blue-black; wing with broad bar of grey-white. Sexes similar; female a little duller than male, with less black around bill. **DISTRIBUTION** W Himalayas, to SE China and Taiwan, discontinuously south to Malay Peninsula; resident. **HABITAT AND HABITS** In Malay Peninsula confined to montane forest above about 1,500m, particularly in middle storey of conifers. At Fraser's Hill it was for many years known only from the garden of High Pines Bungalow, where it frequented planted pine trees; the tiny population was apparently gone by the turn of century, but the species is still known from Genting Highlands, Cameron Highlands and other high mountains. Chews up berries and seeds, and said to take rhododendron nectar.

LIST OF HIGHLAND BIRDS

Common and scientific names mostly follow those used by Gill, F. & Donsker, D. (eds), 2018. IOC World Bird List (v8.1). doi : 10.14344/IOC.ML.8.1, but reconciled with the names and taxonomy used by Eaton et al. (2016) where practicable. Species that in Peninsular Malaysia are characteristically confined to montane forest are highlighted in bold.

ABBREVIATIONS

Regions
FH   Fraser's Hill
CH   Cameron Highlands
GH   Genting Highlands

Status in Regions
R   Resident
M   Migrant
V   Vagrant

Common Name	Scientific Name	FH	CH	GH	Notes and Other Names
ANATIDAE (Ducks and Geese)					
Tufted Duck	*Aythya fuligula*	V			Once netted at night
PHASIANIDAE (Pheasants and Quail)					
Malaysian Hill Partridge	***Arborophila campbelli***	R	R	R	
Long-billed Partridge	*Rhizothera longirostris*	R		R	
Ferruginous Partridge	*Caloperdix oculeus*	R			Hills
Mountain Peacock Pheasant	***Polyplectron inopinatum***	R	R	R	
Blue-breasted Quail	*Synoicus chinensis*	M	RM		*Excalfactoria chinensis* Netted at FH
Red Junglefowl	*Gallus gallus*		R		
COLUMBIDAE (Pigeons and Doves)					
Domestic Pigeon	*Columba livia*	R	R		
Spotted Dove	*Spilopelia chinensis*				
Barred Cuckoo Dove	***Macropygia unchall***	R	R	R	
Little Cuckoo Dove	***Macropygia ruficeps***	R	R	R	
Little Green Pigeon	*Treron olax*	R	R		Netted at FH
Thick-billed Green Pigeon	*Treron curvirostra*	R			
Large Green Pigeon	*Treron capellei*	R			Netted at FH
Yellow-vented Green Pigeon	*Treron seimundi*	R	R		
Wedge-tailed Green Pigeon	***Treron sphenurus***	R	R	R	
Emerald Dove	*Chalcophaps indica*	R	R		
Mountain Imperial Pigeon	***Ducula badia***	R	R	R	
Jambu Fruit Dove	*Ptilinopus jambu*	R	R		
CUCULIDAE (Cuckoos)					
Greater Coucal	*Centropus sinensis*	R			
Lesser Coucal	*Centropus bengalensis*	R			Netted at FH
Raffles's Malkoha	*Rhinortha chlorophaea*	R			
Red-billed Malkoha	*Phaenicophaeus javanicus*	R			
Black-bellied Malkoha	*Phaenicophaeus diardi*	R			

Green-billed Malkoha	*Phaenicophaeus tristis*	R	R	R	
Chestnut-breasted Malkoha	*Phaenicophaeus curvirostris*	R			
Chestnut-winged Cuckoo	*Clamator coromandus*	M	M		Netted at FH
Asian Koel	*Eudynamys scolopaceus*	M			Netted at FH
Little Bronze Cuckoo	*Chrysococcyx minutillus*	R			
Violet Cuckoo	*Chrysococcyx xanthorhynchus*	R			
Banded Bay Cuckoo	*Cacomantis sonneratii*	R			
Plaintive Cuckoo	*Cacomantis merulinus*	R			
Sunda Brush Cuckoo	*Cacomantis sepulcralis*	R			Rusty-breasted Cuckoo
Drongo Cuckoo	*Surniculus lugubris*	RM	RM		
Mountain Hawk-cuckoo	***Hierococcyx bocki***	R	R	R	*Hierococcyx sparverioides* (part)
Whistling Hawk-cuckoo	*Hierococcyx nisicolor*	M			Netted at FH
Sunda Cuckoo	*Cuculus lepidus*	R	R	R	
Indian Cuckoo	*Cuculus micropterus*	RM			
Himalayan Cuckoo	*Cuculus saturatus*	M			
HEMIPROCNIDAE (Treeswifts)					
Grey-rumped Treeswift	*Hemiprocne longipennis*	R	R	R	
Whiskered Treeswift	*Hemiprocne comata*		R	R	
APODIDAE (Swifts)					
Silver-rumped Spinetail	*Rhaphidura leucopygialis*	R		R	
White-throated Needletail	*Hirundapus caudacutus*	M			
Silver-backed Needletail	*Hirundapus cochinchinensis*	M	M		
Brown-backed Needletail	*Hirundapus giganteus*	RM	RM	RM	
Plume-toed Swiftlet	*Collocalia affinis*	R	R	R	White-bellied Swiftlet, Glossy Swiftlet *Collocalia esculenta*
Waterfall Swiftlet	*Hydrochous gigas*	R	R	R	Giant Swiftlet. Netted at FH
Himalayan Swiftlet	*Aerodramus brevirostris*	M	M	M	
Edible-nest Swiftlet	*Aerodramus germani*	R			*Aerodramus fuciphagus*
Asian Palm Swift	*Cypsiurus balasiensis*	R			
Fork-tailed Swift	*Apus pacificus*	M	M	M	
House Swift	*Apus nipalensis*	R	R	R	
PODARGIDAE (Frogmouths)					
Blyth's Frogmouth	*Batrachostomus affinis*	R			Horsfield's Frogmouth *Batrachostomus javensis* (part)
CAPRIMULGIDAE (Nightjars)					
Malaysian Eared Nightjar	*Lyncornis temminckii*	R			*Eurostopodus temminckii*
Grey Nightjar	*Caprimulgus jotaka*	M			*Caprimulgus affinis*
RALLIDAE (Rails and Crakes)					
Band-bellied Crake	*Zapornia paykullii*	M			*Porzana pakullii*. Netted
Red-legged Crake	*Rallina fasciata*	R			Netted
Slaty-legged Crake	*Rallina eurizonoides*	M			Netted
White-breasted Waterhen	*Amaurornis phoenicurus*	RM	RM		
Watercock	*Gallicrex cinerea*	M			Netted
HELIORNITHIDAE (Finfoots)					
Masked Finfoot	*Heliopais personatus*	M			Netted
SCOLOPACIDAE (Sandpipers)					
Eurasian Woodcock	*Scolopax rusticola*	M			Netted
Pintail Snipe	*Gallinago stenura*	M			Netted
Common Sandpiper	*Actitis hypoleucos*		M		

TURNICIDAE (Buttonquail)					
Barred Buttonquail	Turnix suscitator		R		
ARDEIDAE (Herons, Bitterns and Egrets)					
Yellow Bittern	Ixobrychus sinensis	R			Netted
Von Schrenk's Bittern	Ixobrychus eurhythmus	M			Netted
Cinnamon Bittern	Ixobrychus cinnamomeus	R			Netted
Black Bittern	Ixobrychus flavicollis	M			Netted
Purple Heron	Ardea purpurea		R		
Little Egret	Egretta garzetta		R		
Chinese Pond Heron	Ardeola bacchus		M		
Malayan Night Heron	Gorsachius melanolophus	M			
Striated Heron	Butorides striata	RM	RM		Little Heron
ACCIPITRIDAE (Hawks and Eagles)					
Oriental Honey-buzzard	Pernis ruficollis	M	M		Crested Honey-buzzard Pernis ptilorhynchus (part)
Black Baza	Aviceda leuphotes	M	M		
Crested Serpent-eagle	Spilornis cheela	R	R	R	
Bat Hawk	Macheiramphus alcinus	R	R		
Blyth's Hawk-eagle	Nisaetus alboniger	R	R	R	Spizaetus alboniger. Hills
Changeable Hawk-eagle	Nisaetus limnaeetus	R	R		Spizaetus cirrhatus (part)
Rufous-bellied Eagle	Lophotriorchis kienerii	R	R	R	Hieraaetus kienerii
Black Eagle	**Ictinaetus malaiensis**	R	R	R	
Crested Goshawk	Lophospiza trivirgata	R			Accipiter trivirgatus
Chinese Sparrowhawk	Tachyspiza soloensis	M	M	M	Accipiter soloensis
Japanese Sparrowhawk	Tachyspiza gularis	M	M		Accipiter gularis
Eurasian Sparrowhawk	Accipiter nisus	V			
Grey-faced Buzzard	Butastur indicus		M		
White-belled Sea-eagle	Haliaeetus leucogaster	R	R		
Eurasian Buzzard	Buteo buteo	M	M		
Black Kite	Milvus migrans		M		
TYTONIDAE (Barn Owls)					
Oriental Bay Owl	Phodilus badius	R			
Barn Owl	Tyto alba		R		
STRIGIDAE (Typical Owls)					
Brown Hawk-owl	Ninox scutulata	R			
Collared Owlet	**Glaucidium brodiei**	R	R	R	
Reddish Scops-owl	Otus rufescens	R			
Mountain Scops-owl	**Otus spilocephalus**	R	R	R	
Oriental Scops-owl	Otus sunia	M			Netted at FH
Collared Scops-owl	Otus lempiji	R			
Brown Wood-owl	Strix indranee	R	R		Strix leptogrammica (part)
Barred Eagle-owl	Bubo sumatranus	R		R	
TROGONIDAE (Trogons)					
Orange-breasted Trogon	Harpactes oreskios	R	R	R	Hills
Red-headed Trogon	**Harpactes erythrocephalus**	R	R	R	
BUCEROTIDAE (Hornbills)					
Helmeted Hornbill	Rhinoplax vigil	R		R	
Great Hornbill	Buceros bicornis	R		R	
Rhinoceros Hornbill	Buceros rhinoceros	R		R	
Bushy-crested Hornbill	Anorrhinus galeritus	R	R	R	
White-crowned Hornbill	Berenicornis comatus	R			

Wreathed Hornbill	*Rhyticeros undulatus*	R	R	R	
CAPITONIDAE (Barbets)					
Fire-tufted Barbet	***Psilopogon pyrolophus***	R	R	R	
Gold-whiskered Barbet	*Psilopogon chrysopogon*	R	R	R	
Red-throated Barbet	*Psilopogon mystacophanos*	R			
Golden-throated Barbet	***Psilopogon franklinii***	R	R	R	
Black-browed Barbet	***Psilopogon oorti***	R	R	R	
Yellow-crowned Barbet	*Psilopogon henricii*	R			
Blue-eared Barbet	*Psilopogon australis*	R	R	R	
Malayan Brown Barbet	*Caloramphus hayii*	R		R	
PICIDAE (Woodpeckers)					
Rufous Piculet	*Sasia abnormis*	R	R		
Speckled Piculet	***Picumnus innominatus***	R	R	R	
Grey-and-Buff Woodpecker	*Hemicircus concretus*	R			
Bamboo Woodpecker	*Gecinulus viridis*	R		R	Hills
Rufous Woodpecker	*Micropternus brachyurus*	R			
Buff-rumped Woodpecker	*Meiglyptes tristis*	R		R	
Buff-necked Woodpecker	*Meiglyptes tukki*	R			
Banded Woodpecker	*Chrysophlegma miniaceum*	R	R		
Chequer-throated Woodpecker	*Chrysophlegma mentale*	R			
Greater Yellow-naped Woodpecker	***Chrysophlegma flavinucha***	R	R	R	
Crimson-winged Woodpecker	*Picus puniceus*	R		R	
Lesser Yellow-naped Woodpecker	***Picus chlorolophus***	R	R	R	
Grey-headed Woodpecker	***Picus canus***		R		Camerons and Gunung Tahan
Maroon Woodpecker	*Blythipicus rubiginosus*	R	R		
Bay Woodpecker	***Blythipicus pyrrhotis***	R	R	R	
Orange-backed Woodpecker	*Reinwardtipicus validus*	R			
Grey-capped Woodpecker	*Jungipicus canicapillus*	R	R		*Picoides canicapillus, Dendrocopos canicapillus*
ALCEDINIDAE (Kingfishers)					
Oriental Dwarf Kingfisher	*Ceyx rufidorsus*	R	R		
Black-backed Dwarf Kingfisher	*Ceyx erithaca*	M	M		Netted at FH
Common Kingfisher	*Alcedo atthis*	M	M		Netted at FH
Banded Kingfisher	*Lacedo pulchella*	R	R		
Ruddy Kingfisher	*Halcyon coromanda*	RM			Netted at FH
White-throated Kingfisher	*Halcyon smyrnensis*		R		
Black-capped Kingfisher	*Halcyon pileata*	M			Netted at FH
Rufous-collared Kingfisher	*Actenoides concretus*	R			
Collared Kingfisher	*Todiramphus chloris*	R			Netted at FH
MEROPIDAE (Bee-eaters)					
Red-bearded Bee-eater	*Nyctyornis amictus*	R	R	R	
Blue-throated Bee-eater	*Merops viridis*	R	R	R	
Blue-tailed Bee-eater	*Merops philippinus*	M	M		
CORACIIDAE (Dollarbird)					
Dollarbird	*Eurystomus orientalis*	R			
FALCONIDAE (Falcons)					
Black-thighed Falconet	*Microhierax fringillarius*	R	R		
Common Kestrel	*Falco tinnunculus*	M			
Peregrine Falcon	*Falco peregrinus*	RM	RM	RM	
PSITTACIDAE (Parrots)					

Blue-rumped Parrot	Psittinus cyanurus	R			
Blue-crowned Hanging Parrot	Loriculus galgulus	R		R	
EURYLAIMIDAE (Broadbills)					
Long-tailed Broadbill	**Psarisomus dalhousiae**	R	R	R	
Dusky Broadbill	Corydon sumatranus	R			
Silver-breasted Broadbill	**Serilophus lunatus**	R	R	R	
Banded Broadbill	Eurylaimus javanicus	R			
Black-and-Yellow Broadbill	Eurylaimus ochromalus	R	R		
CALYPTOMENIDAE (Green Broadbill)					
Green Broadbill	Calyptomena viridis	R	R		Netted at FH
PITTIDAE (Pittas)					
Rusty-naped Pitta	**Pitta oatesi**	R	R	R	
Blue-winged Pitta	Pitta moluccensis	RM	RM		
Hooded Pitta	Pitta sordida	M			Netted at FH
VIREONIDAE (Vireos)					
Blyth's Shrike-babbler	**Pteruthius aeralatus**	R	R	R	White-browed Shrike-babbler
Black-eared Shrike-babbler	**Pteruthius melanotis**	R	R	R	
White-bellied Erpornis	Erpornis zantholeuca	R	R		White-bellied Yuhina Yuhina zantholeuca
ORIOLIDAE (Orioles)					
Black-and-Crimson Oriole	**Oriolus cruentus**	R	R	R	
Black-hooded Oriole	Oriolus xanthornus	R			
Black-naped Oriole	Oriolus chinensis	RM	RM		
VANGIDAE (Vangas and Allies)					
Bar-winged Flycatcher-shrike	Hemipus picatus	R	R	R	
Black-winged Flycatcher-shrike	Hemipus hirundinaceus	R	R		
Large Woodshrike	Tephrodornis virgatus	R	R		
Maroon-breasted Philentoma	Philentoma velata	R			
AEGITHINIDAE (Ioras)					
Comon Iora	Aegithina tiphia	R			
CAMPEPHAGIDAE (Cuckoo-shrikes and Allies)					
Malaysian Cuckoo-shrike	**Coracina larutensis**	R	R	R	
Lesser Cuckoo-shrike	Lalage fimbriata	R	R		
Fiery Minivet	Pericrocotus igneus	R			
Grey-chinned Minivet	**Pericrocotus solaris**	R	R	R	
Scarlet Minivet	Pericrocotus flammeus	R	R	R	
Ashy Minivet	Pericrocotus divaricatus	M			
RHIPIDURIDAE (Fantails)					
White-throated Fantail	**Rhipidura albicollis**	R	R	R	
DICRURIDAE (Drongos)					
Crow-billed Drongo	Dicrurus annectens	M			
Bronzed Drongo	Dicrurus aeneus	R	R	R	
Lesser Racket-tailed Drongo	**Dicrurus remifer**	R	R	R	
Greater Racket-tailed Drongo	Dicrurus paradiseus	R	R		
MONARCHIDAE (Monarchs)					
Black-naped Monarch	Hypothymis azurea	R			
Japanese Paradise Flycatcher	Terpsiphone atrocaudata	M			
Blyth's Paradise Flycatcher	Terpsiphone affinis	RM	RM		Asian Paradise Flycatcher Terpsiphone paradisi
LANIIDAE (Shrikes)					

Tiger Shrike	*Lanius tigrinus*	M	M	M	
Brown Shrike	*Lanius cristatus*	M	M	M	
Long-tailed Shrike	*Lanius schach*		R		
Jay Shrike	*Platylophus galericulatus*	R			
CORVIDAE (Crows)					
Common Green Magpie	**Cissa chinensis**	R	R	R	
Slender-billed Crow	*Corvus enca*	R			
Southern Jungle Crow	*Corvus macrorhynchos*	R	R	R	
House Crow	*Corvus splendens*		R		
EUPETIDAE (Rail Babbler)					
Rail Babbler	*Eupetes macrocerus*	R			
STENOSTIRIDAE (Fairy Flycatchers)					
Grey-headed Canary-flycatcher	*Culicicapa ceylonensis*	R	R		
PARIDAE (Tits)					
Sultan Tit	*Melanochlora sultanea*	R	R		Hills
HIRUNDINIDAE (Swallows and Martins)					
Asian House Martin	*Delichon dasypus*	M	M	M	
Rufous-bellied Swallow	*Cecropis badia*	R			*Hirundo daurica*
Daurian Swallow	*Cecropis daurica*	M			Striated Swallow *Hirundo daurica, Cecropis striolata*
Pacific Swallow	*Hirundo tahitica*	R	R	R	
Barn Swallow	*Hirundo rustica*	M	M	M	
PYCNONOTIDAE (Bulbuls)					
Ochraceous Bulbul	**Alophoixus ochraceus**	R	R	R	
Buff-vented Bulbul	*Iole charlottae*	R			
Cinereous Bulbul	*Hemixos cinereus*	R	R	R	Ashy Bulbul *Hemixos flavala, Criniger flavala*
Mountain Bulbul	**Ixos mcclellandii**	R	R	R	
Streaked Bulbul	*Ixos malaccensis*	R			
Black-crested Bulbul	*Pycnonotus flaviventris*	R	R	R	*Pycnonotus melanicterus* (part)
Scaly-breasted Bulbul	*Pycnonotus squamatus*	R			
Stripe-throated Bulbul	*Pycnonotus finlaysoni*	R	R	R	Hills
Yellow-vented Bulbul	*Pycnonotus goiavier*	R	R	R	
Olive-winged Bulbul	*Pycnonotus plumosus*	R			
Red-eyed Bulbul	*Pycnonotus brunneus*	R			
Black-headed Bulbul	*Microtarsus atriceps*	R	R		*Pycnonotus atriceps, Brachypodius atriceps*
Black-and-White Bulbul	*Pycnonotus melanoleucos*		R		
TIMALIIDAE (Old World Babblers)					
Striped Tit Babbler	*Mixornis gularis*	R		R	
Golden Babbler	**Cyanoderma chrysaeum**	R	R	R	*Stachyris chrysaea*
Rufous-fronted Babbler	*Cyanoderma rufifrons*	R			
Chestnut-backed Scimitar Babbler	*Pomatorhinus montanus*	R		R	
Large Scimitar Babbler	**Erythrogenys hypoleucos**	R	R	R	
Grey-throated Babbler	*Stachyris nigriceps*	R	R	R	Hills
White-headed Babbler	*Gampsorhynchus torquatus*	R			Collared Babbler, White-hooded Babbler
PELLORNEIDAE (Ground Babblers)					
Moustached Babbler	*Malacopteron magnirostre*	R			

Common Name	Scientific Name				Notes
Rufous-winged Fulvetta	*Schoeniparus castaneceps*	R	R	R	*Alcippe castaneceps*
Buff-breasted Babbler	*Trichastoma tickelli*	R	R	R	
Marbled Wren Babbler	*Turdinus marmoratus*	R		R	*Napothera marmorata*
Streaked Wren Babbler	*Turdinus brevicaudatus*	R	R	R	*Napothera brevicaudata*
Eyebrowed Wren Babbler	*Napothera epilepidota*	R		R	
LEIOTHRICHIDAE (Laughingthrushes)					
Mountain Nun Babbler	*Alcippe peracensis*	R	R	R	
Cutia	*Cutia nipalensis*	R	R	R	
Chestnut-capped Laughingthrush	*Garrulax mitratus*	R	R	R	
Black Laughingthrush	*Garrulax lugubris*	R	R	R	
Chestnut-crowned Laughingthrush	*Trochalopteron erythrocephalum*	R	R	R	*Garrulax erythrocephalus*
Long-tailed Sibia	*Heterophasia picaoides*	R	R	R	
Silver-eared Mesia	*Leiothrix argentauris*	R	R	R	
Blue-winged Minla	*Siva cyanouroptera*	R	R	R	
Bar-throated Minla	*Chrysominla strigula*		R	R	Chestnut-winged Minla *Minla strigula*
ZOSTEROPIDAE (White-eyes)					
Everett's White-eye	*Zosterops everetti*	R	R	R	Hills
PHYLLOSCOPIDAE (Leaf Warblers)					
Yellow-browed Warbler	*Abrornis inornatus*	M	M		*Phylloscopus inornatus*
Two-barred Warbler	*Phylloscopus plumbeitarsus*	V			Netted at FH
Eastern Crowned Leaf Warbler	*Seicercus coronatus*	M			
Chestnut-crowned Leaf Warbler	*Seicercus castaniceps*	R	R	R	
Yellow-breasted Warbler	*Seicercus grammiceps*	R	R	R	*Seicercus montis*
Arctic Warbler	*Seicercus borealis*	M	M	M	
Mountain Leaf Warbler	*Seicercus trivirgatus*	R	R	R	
CETTIDAE (Bush Warblers and Allies)					
Bamboo Bush Warbler	*Abroscopus superciliaris*	R	R	R	Yellow-bellied Warbler
Mountain Leaftoiler	*Phyllergates cucullatus*	R	R	R	Mountain Tailorbird *Orthotomus cucullatus*
PNOEPYGIDAE (Cupwings)					
Pygmy Cupwing	*Pnoepyga pusilla*	R	R	R	Pygmy Wren Babbler
ACROCEPHALIDAE (Marsh and Tree Warblers)					
Oriental Reed Warbler	*Acrocephalus orientalis*	M			Netted at FH
LOCUSTELLIDAE (Grassbirds and Allies)					
Lanceolated Warbler	*Locustella lanceolata*	M	M		Netted at FH
Pallas's Grasshopper Warbler	*Locustella certhiola*	M	M		Netted at FH
CISTICOLIDAE (Cisticolas and Allies)					
Rufescent Prinia	*Prinia rufescens*	R			
Yellow-bellied Prinia	*Prinia flaviventris*	R	R		
Common Tailorbird	*Orthotomus sutorius*	R	R	R	
Dark-necked Tailorbird	*Orthotomus atrogularis*	R	R	R	
SITTIDAE (Nuthatches)					
Velvet-fronted Nuthatch	*Sitta frontalis*	R		R	
Blue Nuthatch	*Sitta azurea*	R	R	R	
STURNIDAE (Starlings)					
Asian Glossy Starling	*Aplonis panayensis*	R			Netted at FH
Daurian Starling	*Agropsar sturninus*	M			Purple-backed Starling *Sturnus sturninus* Netted at FH
Common Myna	*Acridotheres tristis*		R		

TURDIDAE (Thrushes)

White's Thrush	Zoothera aurea	M			Scaly Thrush Zoothera dauma
Siberian Thrush	Geokichla sibirica	M	M	M	Zoothera sibirica
Orange-headed Thrush	Geokichla citrina	M	M		Zoothera citrina
Eyebrowed Thrush	Turdus obscurus	M	M	M	

MUSCICAPIDAE (Old World Flycatchers)

Oriental Magpie Robin	Copsychus saularis	R	R	R	
White-rumped Shama	Kittacincla malabarica	R			
Dark-sided Flycatcher	Muscicapa sibirica	M	M		
Asian Brown Flycatcher	Muscicapa dauurica	M	M	M	
Williamson's Flycatcher	Muscicapa williamsoni	M			Reported seen at FH
Ferruginous Flycatcher	Muscicapa ferruginea	M	M		
Hill Blue Flycatcher	Cyornis caerulatus	R	R	R	Cyornis banyumas. Hills
Blue-throated Blue-flycatcher	Cyornis rubeculoides	M			Netted at FH
Pale Blue Flycatcher	Cyornis unicolor		R		
Brown-chested Jungle Flycatcher	Cyornis brunneatus	M			Rhinomyias brunneatus. Netted at FH
Rufous-browed Flycatcher	**Anthipes solitaris**	R	R	R	Ficedula solitaris
Large Niltava	**Niltava grandis**	R	R	R	
Rufous-bellied Niltava	**Niltava sumatrana**		R		
Blue-and-White Flycatcher	**Cyanoptila cyanomelana**	M	M		
Asian Verditer Flycatcher	Eumyias thalassinus	R	R	R	
Lesser Shortwing	**Brachypteryx leucophris**	R	R	R	
Rufous-headed Robin	**Larvivora ruficeps**		V		Luscinia ruficeps. Netted once
Siberian Blue Robin	Larvivora cyane	M			
Chestnut-naped Forktail	Enicurus ruficapillus	R		R	
Slaty-backed Forktail	**Enicurus schistaceus**	R	R	R	
Malayan Whistling Thrush	**Myophonus robinsoni**	R	R	R	
Blue Whistling Thrush	Myophonus caeruleus	RM	RM	RM	
Siberian Rubythroat	Calliope calliope	M			Netted at FH
White-tailed Robin	**Myiomela leucura**	R	R		
Little Pied Flycatcher	**Ficedula westermanni**	R	R	R	
Snowy-browed Flycatcher	**Ficedula hyperythra**	R	R	R	
Mugimaki Flycatcher	Ficedula mugimaki	M	M	M	
Yellow-rumped Flycatcher	Ficedula zanthopygia	M			Netted at FH
Pygmy Blue Flycatcher	**Ficedula hodgsoni**	R	R		Muscicapella hodgsoni
White-throated Rock Thrush	Monticola gularis	M			
Blue Rock Thrush	Monticola solitarius	RM			

CHLOROPSEIDAE (Leafbirds)

Greater Green Leafbird	Chloropsis sonnerati	R			
Lesser Green Leafbird	Chloropsis cyanopogon	R			
Orange-bellied Leafbird	**Chloropsis hardwickii**	R	R	R	
Blue-winged Leafbird	Chloropsis cochinchinensis	R	R	R	

IRENIDAE (Fairy Bluebirds)

Asian Fairy Bluebird	Irena puella	R	R	R	

DICAEIDAE (Flowerpeckers)

Yellow-breasted Flowerpecker	Prionochilus maculatus	R		R	
Scarlet-breasted Flowerpecker	Prionochilus thoracicus	R			
Crimson-breasted Flowerpecker	Prionochilus percussus	R	R	R	

Yellow-vented Flowerpecker	*Dicaeum chrysorrheum*	R		R	*Pachyglossa chrysorrhea*
Thick-billed Flowerpecker	*Dicaeum agile*	R			*Pachyglossa modesta*
Orange-bellied Flowerpecker	*Dicaeum trigonostigma*	R		R	
Plain Flowerpecker	*Dicaeum minullum*	R			*Dicaeum concolor*
Scarlet-backed Flowerpecker	*Dicaeum cruentatum*	R	R		
Fire-breasted Flowerpecker	***Dicaeum ignipectus***	R	R	R	Buff-bellied Flowerpecker
NECTARINIIDAE (Sunbirds and Spiderhunters)					
Ruby-cheeked Sunbird	*Chalcoparia singalensis*	R			
Plain Sunbird	*Anthreptes simplex*	R			
Black-throated Sunbird	***Aethopyga saturata***	R	R	R	
Temminck's Sunbird	*Aethopyga temminckii*	R	R		
Thick-billed Spiderhunter	*Arachnothera crassirostris*	R	R		
Long-billed Spiderhunter	*Arachnothera robusta*	R	R		
Little Spiderhunter	*Arachnothera longirostra*	R	R	R	
Yellow-eared Spiderhunter	*Arachnothera chrysogenys*	R	R		
Streaked Spiderhunter	***Arachnothera magna***	R	R	R	
Spectacled Spiderhunter	*Arachnothera flavigaster*	R			
Grey-breasted Spiderhunter	*Arachnothera modesta*	R			
Purple-naped Spiderhunter	*Arachnothera hypogrammica*	R			*Hypogramma hypogrammicum* *Kurochkinegramma hypogrammicum*
ESTRILDIDAE (Estrildid Finches)					
Pin-tailed Parrotfinch	*Erythrura prasina*	R		R	Hills
Tawny-breasted Parrotfinch	*Erythrura hyperythra*		R		Hills
White-rumped Munia	*Lonchura striata*	R	R	R	
Scaly-breasted Munia	*Lonchura punctulata*	R	R		
PASSERIDAE (Old World Sparrows)					
Eurasian Tree Sparrow	*Passer montanus*	R	R		
MOTACILLIDAE (Wagtails and Pipits)					
Forest Wagtail	*Dendronanthus indicus*	M			
Yellow Wagtail	*Motacilla flava*	M			Netted at FH
Grey Wagtail	*Motacilla cinerea*	M	M	M	
White Wagtail	*Motacilla alba*	M			
Olive-backed Pipit	*Anthus hodgsoni*	M	M	M	
Paddyfield Pipit	*Anthus rufulus*	R	R	R	
FRINGILLIDAE (True Finches)					
Brown Bullfinch	***Pyrrhula nipalensis***	R	R	R	

REFERENCES

Bransbury, J. 1993. *A Birdwatcher's Guide to Malaysia*. Waymark Publishing.

Chua, L. S. L. & Saw, L. G. 2001. A reassessment of the flora of Gunung Ulu Kali, Genting Highlands, Malaysia – preliminary findings and trends. *Malayan Nature Journal* 55: 65–76.

Davison, G. W. H. & Yeap, C. A. *A Naturalist's Guide to the Birds of Malaysia and Singapore*. John Beaufoy Publishing, Oxford.

Eaton, J. A., van Balen, B., Brickle, N. W. & Rheindt, F. A. 2016. *Birds of the Indonesian Archipelago. Greater Sundas and Wallacea*. Lynx Edicions, Barcelona.

Jeyarajasingam, A. & Pearson, A. 1999. *A Field Guide to Birds of Peninsular Malaysia and Singapore*. Oxford: Oxford University Press.

Kiew, R. 1998. The seed plants at Fraser's Hill. Peninsular Malaysia with special reference to its conservation status. Forestry Research Institute Malaysia, Kepong. *Research Pamphlets* 121: 173–210.

Lee, T. M., Soh, M. C., Sodhi, N., Koh, L. P. & Lim, S. L. H. 2005. Effects of habitat disturbance on mixed species bird flocks in a tropical sub-montane rainforest. *Biological Conservation* 122(2): 193–204.

Leong, T. M., Murphy, P. V., Gan, C. W., D'Rozario, V. & Strange, B. C. 2017. *Marvellous Moths of Fraser's Hill and Other Highlands of Peninsular Malaysia: a Photographic Memoir*. Singapore.

McClure, H. E. 1964. Avian bionomics in Malaya. I. The avifauna above 5000 feet altitude at Mount Brinchang, Pahang. *Bird Banding* 35: 141–183.

Medway, Lord & Wells, D. R. 1976. *The Birds of the Malay Peninsula*. Vol. 5. Conclusion and survey of every species. Witherby, London.

Norhayati, A., A. D. Farah, K. O. Chan, B. Daicus & Muin, M. A. 2011. An update of herpetofaunal records from Bukit Fraser, Pahang, Peninsular Malaysia. *Malaysian Applied Biology Journal* 40: 9–17.

Peh, K. S.-H. 2009. Potential effects of climate change on elevational distributions of tropical birds in Southeast Asia. *Condor* 109(2): 43–441.

Peh, K. S-H., Soh, M. C. K., Sodhi, N. S., Laurance, W. F., Ong, D. J. & Clements, R. 2011. Up in the clouds: is sustainable use of tropical montane cloud forests possible in Malaysia? *BioScience* 61(1): 27–38.

Peh, K. S. H., Soh, M. C., Yap, C. A. M. & Sekercioglu, C. H. 2012. Correlates of elevational specialisation in Southeast Asian tropical birds. *Raffles Bulletin of Zoology* 249–257.

REACH. 2014. *Montane Birds of Cameron Highlands*. Regional Environmental Awareness Cameron Highlands, Brinchang, Malaysia.

Robson, C. 2008. *A Field Guide to the Birds of South-east Asia*. New Holland, London.

Soh, M. C., Sodhi, N. S. & Lim, S. L. 2006. High sensitivity of montane bird communities to habitat disturbance in Peninsular Malaysia. *Biological Conservation* 129(2): 149–166.

Strange, M. 2004. *Birds of Fraser's Hill: an Illustrated Guide and Checklist*. Nature's Niche Pte Ltd., Singapore.

Tan, M. K. & Khairul Nizam, K. 2014. *Orthoptera of Fraser's Hill, Peninsular Malaysia*. Lee Kong Chian Museum of Natural History, National University of Singapore. e-book available at http://lkcnhm.nus.edu.sg.

Thi, B., Lee, S. S., Zainuddin, N. & Chan, H. T. 2011. *A Guidebook to the Macrofungi of Fraser's Hill*. Forest Research Institute Malaysia, Kepong.

Wells, D. R. 1999. *The Birds of the Thai-Malay Peninsula*, Vol. 1. Non-Passerines. Academic Press, London.

Wells, D. R. 2007. *The Birds of the Thai-Malay Peninsula*, Vol. 2. Passerines, A. & C. Black, London.

Accommodation

Following conversion of the 1880s bridle path into a motorable access road after the First World War, the first major wave of Fraser's Hill construction was in the 1920s and '30s. Bungalows such as Arundel and Bunge on the Selangor side, and Buona Vista, Clifford (Jelai), Dacres (Brinchang) and others on the Pahang side were the result. A few more followed in the next decades. The next major wave was sale of land for big corporate resort bungalows (Maybank, Petronas and others) and a few private houses in the late 1960s and early '70s, as well as one hotel, the Merlin (now Shahzan Inn). Following construction of Puncak Inn at the town centre, in the 1990s major resorts were built at Silverpark (private apartments) and Fraser's Pine Resort (hotel). There is no guarantee that the following details are still valid; bungalows open and close, and phone numbers often change. Fraser's Hill Development Corporation is the key agency with stability and ability to advise on the current situation. Stephen's Place is the most nature orientated of the accommodation possibilities.

Fraser's Hill Development Corporation (FHDC)
Enquiries: (+6)09 3622195 / 3622084 (office),
3622201 (information centre)
Email: pkbf2006@yahoo.com, pkbf@streamyx.com
Web: www.pkbf.org.my

Stephen's Place (Buona Vista Bungalow)
Enquiries: (+6)013 8185760
Web: www.stephens-place.co.uk

Agrobank Bungalow (Bank Pertanian Malaysia)
Enquiries: (+6)03 89259042 /43, /44, /45
Email: amu@agrobank.com.my
Web: www.agrobank.com.my, facebook/Agrobank

TM Resort, Peninjau Apartments
Enquiries: (+6)09 3622500 / 3622400, 018 3782103
(bungalow), 017 9482413 (Peninjau)
Web: www.bph.gov.my

Sri Berkat Rest House (Selangor Tourism)
Enquiries: (+6)03 5513200 (weekdays), 09 3622036
or 013 9068075 (weekends)
Web: www.sriberkat.weebly.com

Shahzan Inn, Jalan Lady Guillemard
Enquiries: (+6)09 3622300

Arundel Bungalow & Bunge Bungalow
(KLK Holiday Bungalows Sdn Bhd)
Enquiries: (+6)05 2417844
Email: holidaybungalow@klk.com.my

Puncak Inn
Enquiries: (+6)09 3622056

Abu Suradi, Hollebekke (Cini) & The Cottage
(Bintang) Bungalows
Tourism Pahang
Enquiries: (+6)09 3622007
Email: puncakinn2@yahoo.com

Silverpark Holiday Apartments
Enquiries: (+6)09 3622888;
(+6)0326924781/26924782, (+6)0326916633 ext 863

The Smokehouse Hotel & Restaurant, Jalan Jeriau
Enquiries: (+6)09 3622226

Fraser's Pine Resort
Enquiries: (+6)09 3622122

Pekan Bungalow, Jalan Lady Guillemard
Enquiries: (+6)09 3622645 or (+6)03 21644191
Email: sales@rezabmutiara.com
Web: www.rezabmutiara.com

A nature guide based in Fraser's Hill is:

K. S. Durai
Enquiries: (+6)013 9831633
Email: durefh@hotmail.com
Web: facebook.co/duraibirdman